BEHIND
the
OFFSHORE VEIL

by
Jeffrey H. Corbett & Patrick J. Kish

iUniverse, Inc.
New York   Bloomington

iUniverse books may be ordered through booksellers or by contacting:

iUniverse
1663 Liberty Drive
Bloomington, IN 47403
www.iuniverse.com
1-800-Authors (1-800-288-4677)

ISBN: 978-1-4401-4663-3 (sc)
ISBN: 978-1-4401-4661-9 (dj)
ISBN: 978-1-4401-4662-6 (ebook)

Printed in the United States of America

iUniverse rev. date: 05/14/2009

Dedication

To my wife Cindy, who lovingly supported this effort.
You had faith in my abilities and potential long before I did.
Also to my late Mother and Father who guided me through life
with their love and support.

Jeff Corbett

To Jean and Greg, you are my inspiration.
Also to Jeff, thank you for the last seventeen years.

Pat Kish

Preface

This book is the product of a unique collaboration, written by two authors who attempt to offer insightful observations regarding the practical applications of the offshore industry. In particular, what can legally and ethically be accomplished by owning a private financial institution including a Private Bank and/or Trust Company.

We admit our bias ahead of time. As the principal owners of Worldwide Business Consultants, Inc., we have a vested interest in the concept. You should keep that in mind when reading this material. It is also true, however, that if we did not believe in the validity of the concept, our business interests would be pursued elsewhere.

There is nothing illegal, immoral or unpatriotic about doing business offshore. Business has been conducted in this manner prior to the birth of the United States and certainly no end is in sight. English trust law itself, often referred to as the mainstay of the offshore market, can easily be traced back more than 400 years.

Private International Banking is a very old and universally recognized business endeavor. Politics and international business, however, cannot be separated. Therefore, it is important for those who would consider this path to understand the political ramifications. During a period of time when in many nations, including the United States, the strongest lobbyists successfully affect the largest amount of legislation, it offers the non-politician a meaningful "extra" vote. This same technique has been utilized by dissatisfied merchants and business people for centuries. Simply stated, it involves taking your wallet with its contents and moving those assets elsewhere.

Ownership of an offshore financial institution cannot be used as a tax shelter and should not be approached with the hopes of attaining any such related perks. In most instances, domestic controls have been implemented to curb any such benefits. Offshore banking is however, a wonderful entrepreneurial opportunity that when used correctly can provide the highest possible profit potential in addition to increasing privacy and asset protection for those parties involved.

The pragmatic applications of doing business offshore are many. Often opportunities are only limited by personal imagination and budgetary restraints. Obviously, domestic hurdles can be encountered but any restriction attempted to be placed on international commerce always has serious repercussions. The contents of this book are meant to serve as an informative overview into the world of offshore banking. It is our sincere hope that you find it an enjoyable and enlightening read.

About the Authors

Jeffrey H. Corbett

Jeffrey H. Corbett co-founded Worldwide Business Consultants, Inc., in 1991 and has held the position of President since the company's inception. He also serves as Editor, Co-Publisher and frequent contributor to C&K Magazine (formerly Vision Magazine), a product of Corbett & Kish Publishing founded in 1999. In addition, he co-authored the acclaimed book, Behind the Offshore Veil, Understanding Private Bank Ownership.

With over twenty years experience in the financial marketplace, Jeffrey Corbett has served in various significant capacities throughout the industry. In 1980, he joined a firm specializing in deferred compensation. He was quickly promoted to Director of Marketing, responsible for implementing and marketing a retirement program for the city of Pittsburgh.

Jeffrey Corbett has maintained a unique and diversified investment industry background joining Dean Witter Reynolds Inc. as a Stockbroker in 1984 and then in 1986 became a member of the firm of Kidder Peabody & Co. As an investment professional, Mr. Corbett specialized in equity strategies involving blue chip, multinational concerns. His perspectives regarding financial markets could frequently be heard on a major radio station or as a much demanded public speaker.

In addition to his professional background, Jeffrey Corbett also serves numerous philanthropies and alumni organizations, recognized both locally and nationally. He co-founded the Los Angeles Chapter of the Buoniconti Fund to Cure Paralysis in 1997. He is also a member of the University of Pittsburgh's Phi Delta Theta Alumni Chapter as well as the Kentucky Colonels Association.

Patrick J. Kish

Patrick J. Kish co-founded Worldwide Business Consultants in 1991 and has held the position of CEO since the company's inception. He is responsible for guiding thousands of clients to successfully establish global business endeavors. He also serves as Co-Publisher and frequent contributor of C&K Magazine (formerly Vision Magazine), a product of Corbett & Kish Publishing, founded in 1999. In addition, he co-authored the acclaimed book, Behind the Offshore Veil, Understanding Private Bank Ownership.

Patrick Kish has a broad range of diverse business experience that uniquely qualifies him to serve as CEO of Worldwide Business Consultants, Inc. In the earlier stages of his career, he served in a management capacity with a few of the largest entertainment concerns in Los Angeles. This exposure has provided Patrick Kish the opportunity to gain an understanding for the unique problems associated with high profile clients. In each position, he implemented programs that significantly increased sales, employee retention and enhanced corporate image. In the mid-eighties, his career focused more sharply on the financial industries which culminated when Patrick Kish was named Executive Vice President of an international investment concern.

In addition to his professional background, Patrick Kish is also involved in numerous charitable organizations recognized both locally and nationally. He served as a Founding Board Member of the Los Angeles Chapter of the Buonconti Fund to Cure Paralysis in 1997. In addition he frequently donates his time to the Los Angeles Mission and sponsors underprivileged children and their families during the Holiday season.

Forward

Please Pay Your Taxes ... Please!!!

Wesley Snipes seems like a nice person. We have always found his movies entertaining (more the older, "White Men Can't Jump" film as opposed to the "Blade" series). But Mr. Snipes may have gotten himself in over his head when he apparently became involved with what federal prosecutors deem to be a tax protestor group out of Florida. As he quickly found out, being naïve is not a defense, and he was recently sentenced to three years for willfully failing to file tax returns. Mr. Snipes, who was convicted in February, received one year for each count, to be served consecutively and an additional year of probation. An appeal is expected.

"Taxes are what we pay for a civilized society."
- Oliver Wendall Holmes quote inscribed over the entrance to the Internal Revenue Services Building in Washington D.C.

California billionaire Igor Olenicoff has had his problems. According to a recent Wall Street Journal article, Mr. Olenicoff is cooperating with investigators in a widening probe that involves the Private Banking Group of UBS - This after the former Russian immigrant entered a guilty plea last December to the charge of filing false tax returns in 2002 and was ordered to pay $52 million.

Can't we all just get along? A recent Forbes Magazine article points to the wealthy using offshore vehicles not for tax evasion but for personal asset protection and to open new avenues of business. Finally, a major financial periodical called out the attorney behind the frivolous lawsuit as the major threat to wealth, not the taxman. We applaud this article. Look, we all want to pay less tax, but to us this is a no-brainer.

Just consider the risk vs. reward ratio at illegally using the offshore market to hide money or becoming part of a fringe tax protesting group. You will get caught. Besides, the real threat, which is the attorney looking for deep pockets, is not being addressed by these senseless actions.

"If the blind lead the blind, both shall fall into a ditch."
- Matthew 15:14

Lowering your financial profile through the use of offshore vehicles thus making it harder for a recent law school graduate to earn his or her chops makes sense; best of all, it is legal. Who knows? You may even open new avenues for your business interests along the way. As the old TV commercial tag line once read, "try it - you'll like it."

Table of Contents

Chapter 1

"The United States is an Offshore Banking Center"

- *Offshore Bank*

A bank located outside the country of residence of either the depositor or owner.

- *Edge Act Corporation*

A federally-chartered U.S. corporation that is only allowed to engage in international banking or other financial transactions related to international business. Authority was established by the Edge Act in 1919. The International Banking Act of 1978 allows foreign banks to own Edge Act corporations.

- *International Banking Facilities (IBFs)*

Institutions in the United States that allow depository (banks) to offer services to foreign residents and institutions free of some Federal Reserve requirements and some state and local income taxes.

"Let every man know thee, but let no man know thee thoroughly."

- Ben Franklin

Banking is the Business of Moving Money for Profit.

The world economy is a very competitive market where businesses vie for profit and governments compete for capital. Nations often engage in activities far more fiercely aggressive than the largest corporations. Being states of government provides them the means to an extensive arsenal of tools which can be utilized against opponents in an economic game of "Risk."

"Foreign investors now hold more than 55% of the publicly-held and-traded U.S. Treasury securities. These assets come to the U.S. for security, tax-free investment and privacy. Overseas wealth inflow now plays a critical role in the U.S. economy by bridging the gap between domestic supplies of capital and demand for it."
- *US Department of Treasury*

Actions can be obvious, such as defensive legislation, or may only involve a passing diplomatic conversation implying the threat of policy change. From tariffs on manufactured goods to restrictions on currency, the nations of the world compete for your assets. Since banking is the business of moving money for profit, it follows that politics are interwoven into the very fabric of that industry. Nothing seems to bring politicians and bureaucrats to the bully pulpit quicker than the subject of international banking, which includes its proverbial redheaded stepchild, offshore banking.

A strong banking system is a sign of a sturdy economy. Governments need a thriving economy since it adds to their powerbase and stability. Just like entrepreneurship, either you grow or you die. Therefore, a balancing act occurs between the need for international growth and the need for protectionism. Nations, however, cannot exist in a fiscal vacuum; they need other governments to be trading partners. Even mighty nations, those that may attempt to have their cake and eat it too, must walk this tightrope. As a result, an inherent conflict exists.

The Perception Game (Offshore is a Dirty Word)

In today's global economy, trillions of dollars move each day. How and where those funds get invested is the focal point of the heated competition we have been discussing; public opinion can influence those decisions. Therefore, international banking and its image have never been more important, and creating a negative connotation about an industry or a country serves a purpose.

At some point in time, our business vernacular changed, and "offshore" became a dirty word. This was not always the case-the irony being that offshore financial markets thrive. Consider the Cayman Islands: as of 2003, more than 68,000 companies were registered there including almost 500 banks, 800 insurers, and 5,000 mutual funds. A stock exchange was opened in 1997. Often viewed as a refuge for tax evaders and drug lords, the tiny country is an overseas territory of the UK and home to some of the best known names in American banking including Citibank, Bank of America, Wells Fargo and many others. Why would these major banks with billions of dollars in deposits and reputations at stake want to set up shop in an island nation? The simple answer is profit. Why would territories of the United Kingdom, one of the United States closest allies, permit a haven to exist for ill-gotten gains? Simply stated, they don't. The banking infrastructure of the Cayman Islands is no more good or evil than any other, and this surely holds true in a post 9-11 world market. With no direct taxation and a system that respects the privacy of their depositors, the Cayman Islands are able to successfully compete in the international arena.

This does not mean that you can run to the islands to hide from the taxman. It will not work, and you will likely have a difficult time opening an account if you are a US citizen. Perception in the United States of both this country and the offshore financial markets in general tends to be very different from reality.

"Contrary to the popular vision of "offshore" banking, the true purpose of these accounts for many wealth clients is to protect a lifetime of earnings and savings not from being taxed, but from being wiped out in a major lawsuit."

- Forbes Magazine

The US Competes for FDI

As a rule of thumb, the United States welcomes foreign investment, (often referred to as FDI or Foreign Direct Investment) with relatively very few restrictions except for a historical ebb and flow of policy decisions involving national security. Basically, the exporting of goods and the importing of currency are encouraged while, conversely, the importing of goods and exporting of currency are discouraged.

In 1988 the Rolling Stones explained why they left England to Washington Post writer, Richard Harrington, for his article entitled "Stone Free." -

"In 1971, we were forced to make a decision courtesy of the British government - live in England and (because of high taxes) not be able to afford another set of guitar strings or move and keep the band together. Hence, the album "Exile on Main Street"

The United States has a history of enacting legislation to provide export encouragement or industrial incentives. Tax deferrals or exemptions have been granted to corporations that meet established guidelines. In addition, there are numerous other incentives that has put in place United States' government to attract foreign investment. This is commonplace throughout the world. These "tax holidays" are believed to create new jobs within the country and increase exports. One such tax benefit was the legislation that provided for the establishment of "Foreign Sales Corporations," also known as "Fisks" or "FSCs."

FSCs were a tax incentive authorized under the Deficit Reduction Act of 1984 and manifested in the Internal Revenue Code. Few are aware of their existence, but Foreign Sales Corporations were recognized and endorsed by the US Commerce Department. This tax benefit formerly extended to US manufacturing companies offered a reduction in federal income taxes for profits derived from exports and directed through an offshore subsidiary. The use of FSCs was finally stopped after claims of unfair trade practices were made by EU and upheld by the WTO. Foreign Sales Corporations are a definitive point in time when US policy actually endorsed the use of offshore havens and corporations.

Offshore Banking in the U.S.

Are you aware that foreigners investing in the United States earn tax free interest on bank CDs? In addition, any effort to share this information with other governments for their own tax purposes is illegal. It is true, and, by definition, that fact makes the United States an offshore tax and banking haven.

"My fortune is in the Bahamas Islands and it's going to stay there as long as that bastard is in the White House"

- Quote attributed to an American financier speaking about then President Roosevelt during a period of high tax.

Since the Revenue Act of 1921, Congress has emphasized a U.S. policy of attracting capital to the American economy by not taxing interest paid to non-resident aliens for bank deposits. Law makers have reinforced this position a number of times with the most notable being the Tax Reform Acts of 1976 and 1986. Three days before the end of the Clinton Administration, in an effort to compel a policy change and establish information sharing with foreign tax services, the IRS proposed a regulation to force banks to report this interest. Reaction from Capitol Hill and the financial services industry was swift and firmly opposed to any such move.

According to the U.S. Department of Commerce, at the end of the year 2000, private foreign investment in the U.S. totaled approximately $9 trillion, with $1.8 trillion held in bank deposits. It was feared that any effort to report or directly tax this capital would cause it to take flight to another friendlier jurisdiction and essentially cripple the US banking industry. Today's market has similar numbers.

The U.S. not only acts as a tax haven for fixed income depositors but licenses two banking entities that are virtually identical to the classic definition of an offshore bank. Edge Corporations and International Banking Facilities (see previous definitions) are shell banking units that present ownership with the benefits of being a bank with reduced regulation and lower reserve requirements. To those who would own an offshore banking entity, these facilities provide entrée into the U.S. and the prestige that comes with it.

"A right is not what someone gives you; it's what no one can take from you."

- Ramsey Clark

Conclusion

Virtually every nation in the world competes in the offshore market place for foreign capital. Economic realities make this a necessity for continued national growth, and it is unlikely to change. Those who have something to gain from restricting free enterprise frequently paint the offshore world as evil. In general, however, this market is neither good nor bad but a result of free societies conducting trade.

Chapter 2

"The History of Tax Havens"

The phrase tax haven is often considered to be synonymous with offshore financial centers. In this day of worldwide income tax, however, there are important differences. More to the point, tax haven is actually an outdated term. While it may be possible for multinational corporations to structure their dealings in such a way as to benefit from jurisdictional tax relief, it is rarely possible for an individual to do so. Even so, we thought it important to provide a historic perspective to the term tax haven which follows in this chapter. Just as with any financial endeavor, there are those who would seek to utilize the privileges of these facilities for illegal reasons such as tax evasion. It is important to reiterate that, generally speaking, the amount of tax planning that can be accomplished through offshore entities is minimal and best done by an experienced, international tax professional. Further, it is critical to understand the difference between an avoidance strategy and tax evasion. Tax avoidance is the legal utilization of tax legislation and/or investment vehicles in order to reduce the amount of tax that is payable. By contrast, tax evasion is the general term for illegal efforts not to pay taxes that extend outside of the law.

Tax havens are not easily defined. They have traditionally come in all shapes and sizes, each differing according to their own culture and the type of capital they wish to attract. It is nearly impossible to provide a specific definition that will not result in the exclusion of an important participant. Clouding the picture even further is the fact that governments commonly make

"The tax on capital gains directly affects investment decisions, the mobility and flow of risk capital... the ease or difficulty experienced by new ventures in obtaining capital, and thereby the strength and potential for growth in the economy."
- John F. Kennedy

individual concessions to large corporations in order to create jobs and bring in industry. Grants, loans or tax holidays are frequent enticements offered to these types of entities on an individual project basis.

Generally speaking, tax havens have fallen into one of two broad categories defined as either "low tax" havens or "no tax" havens.

A "Low" Tax Haven - is defined as one in which local income tax would apply to business transacted within its domestic borders but not to foreign source income. So, in other words, business transacted outside the jurisdiction is exempt from any tax.

A "No" Tax Haven - is defined as a country that is totally exempt from corporate and personal income tax. Business can be transacted both domestically and internationally without tax ramifications. There is, however, usually a nominal, annual stamp duty collected by the government that is determined by the capitalization of the company.

In addition, there are three main geographic areas that are commonly recognized for having nations that would fit these parameters. The Caribbean is best known for offering a tropical atmosphere. Its proximity to the United States has proven advantageous. Up until the early 1960's, it was common place and perfectly legal for wealthy Americans to place cash here while on vacation and thus out of the reach of the tax man. The South Pacific is a lesser known area but still a major presence, especially with Asian investors. Finally, Europe has several countries that represent the oldest and most respected havens of the world.

Tax

To comprehend tax havens, one must first start with a basic knowledge of tax. It may be surprising to discover that taxes date back more than 5,000 years. Virtually every society that has ever existed established a tax system. Unfortunately, throughout the course of history, tyranny and terror have been frequently linked to the collection of these taxes. Thus, the desire to avoid tyrannical behavior created the basic mindset to seek refuge in havens.

Ancient Egypt taxed as early as 3,000 B.C. Within their system, the Pharaoh empowered Scribes who were enormously powerful tax collectors. It was not uncommon to find scenes depicting the Scribe's often ruthless actions in Egyptian drawings. Later, during the Roman period, revenue chests of the Roman Senate were greatly enriched by taxing conquered territories. "In this same era, hordes of Roman taxpayers went over to the Barbarians to avoid Rome's oppressive tax enslavement. During the seventh and eighth centuries Islam was considered a tax haven to the Christians. More recently, the first tax haven in the post-medieval world was America. Historians readily acknowledge that more people fled to the new world to avoid Europe's hated the new taxes than for religious or political or political freedom."[1]

"Taxes are what we pay for a civilized society."
- Oliver Wendell Holmes' quote inscribed over the entrance to the Internal Revenue Services Building in Washington D.C.

Many of the present day tax havens, commonly located in the Caribbean and South Pacific, are former British Empire territories. It was not rare for British aristocrats to seek asylum for their wealth in far-away lands. In fact, most would agree that British trust law, the foundation of most modern day tax haven legislation, dates back a minimum of 400 hundred years.

---

[1]Charles Adams, "For Good and Evil, The Impact of Taxes on the Course of Civilization", p. 407

"The trust concept originated in England and transplanted to The Cayman Islands in 1727 with accession of King George II to the throne."[2] From there it spread throughout the British Colonies.

"The power of taxing people and their property is essential to the very existence of government."
- James Madison,
U.S. President

Rising tax rates and an increase in currency controls by one government invariably result in another opening its doors wider to foreign investment. This is the essence of a tax haven. First and foremost, it provides a safe harbor. "A tax haven is a place of shelter or refuge from taxes, particularly high income taxes and death duties. It is not material whether a country is a tax haven by accident or by design. Some countries are tax havens simply because they never got around to imposing taxes."[3] These countries typically have stamp or sales tax in place of income tax.

Tax havens have provided much more than a harbor for those wishing to avoid excessive tax. Political flight capital may even be a greater reason for their existence. History is full of examples of countries providing the wealthy with relief from tyranny, real or perceived, in their homeland. A synopsis of the two most well known havens provides an important perspective for your consideration.

---

[2]"Offshore Outlook," Volume 3, Issue 33, Aug.-Sep., 1995
[3]Marshall J. Langer, "Practical International Tax Planning", p.14

Hong Kong

Hong Kong offers the most recent example where this activity has been chronicled. After more than 150 years of British rule, Hong Kong reverted back to the Chinese on July 1, 1997, causing grave concern about its future. Millions of dollars became flight capital and left this location. Canada has been a huge benefactor of this exodus. Many investors not only moved their money but established second citizenships in this North American location.

Hong Kong is also interesting because it is an example of how the offshore world can change. Prior to 1841, it was an island with a tiny population of approximately 3,000. Hong Kong became a textbook case of a nation short on natural resources; where poverty and crime could have easily over run this nation. Instead, low taxes and nonintervention in business became a source of enormous prosperity. By embracing this "laissez-faire" philosophy, Hong Kong positioned itself for the long term success it enjoyed.

Hong Kong's promise as a business friendly city-state may be suspect, but the historical impact this enormous haven has made is not. Its strategic location in the Asian Pacific region has resulted in it becoming one of busiest harbors in the world and the third largest financial center, behind only New York and London The Sino-British Joint Declaration, signed by both Great Britain and China in 1984 provides for a policy of "one country, two systems" until 2047. In theory, the free-market system is not expected to be affected.

Switzerland

No discussion of tax haven history would be complete without referring to Switzerland. This charming European tax haven is frequently the jurisdiction of choice for those looking for a secure and private location to keep their nest egg.

Switzerland has positioned itself as one of the world's major financial centers by virtue of political stability and economic strength. It is often regarded as the world's premier tax haven. For most people, the mention of offshore investment will immediately create images of the famous Swiss numbered accounts. The mythology of this private Swiss account truly precedes any discussion of tax havens. In this regard, as is often the case, fact and fiction are blurred together.

Numbered accounts are rarely used and often discouraged by high fees. A depositor's financial affairs are secret by law; these accounts are seen as being excessive. This country's central European geographic location, combined with the trustworthiness of Swiss banks, has sustained its tradition for more than one hundred years. Swiss banks currently manage about one third of all privately invested assets worldwide- approximately US$1 trillion. Bank secrecy is a centuries old tradition. For the most part, even the government cannot obtain bank information unless a Swiss court has evidence that a crime has been committed.

As strange as it might seem, in Switzerland tax evasion is not a criminal matter. This not only includes evading foreign income tax but Swiss tax as well. If a Swiss citizen is caught evading local tax, he or she is likely to receive a series of very polite letters from the government requesting his or her cooperation. This frequently leads to a mutually satisfactory joint settlement. Harsh tactics that might be utilized elsewhere are simply not a consideration.

The United States Perspective

As with any generalization, there are exceptions, but for the most part, US perspectives pertaining to the offshore market tend to differ from the perspectives of the rest of the world. Most Americans have adopted an ultra conservative stance. The "offshore market" is viewed with much skepticism often resulting in condemnation. Because of ignorance, this fear of the unknown can result in missed opportunity, lack of proper asset protection planning or poor estate preparation. All of these problems could be easily avoided with an open mind and basic education. Over the years we have discovered that the foundation for this rationale is basically established within a group of six primary issues. Fallacy and fact are inseparable within this reasoning.

"The income tax has made liars out of more Americans than golf."
- Will Rogers

1)   **"Geography"** - The United States has a very distinctive and powerful geographic presence. From its early history forward, the economic advantage of "Manifest Destiny" was not lost on entrepreneurs and politicians alike. This "coast to coast" presence was unmatched in Europe and provided a gateway for trade. Large natural resource reserves, complimented by political stability and freedom, provided the needed edge over the Far East. Thus, a superpower evolved with a mindset of self sufficiency. Isolationism, defined as purposely avoiding political or economic interaction with other nations, developed into a popular stance. Until recent history, most citizens perceived no urgent need to look overseas. Consequently, the geography of the United States lent a hand early on with the majority of the US population becoming unfamiliar with foreign lands.

2)   **"Buy American"** - In the mid to late 1970's, the cry to "buy American" became very common among the United States middle class. Most credit the automobile industry to be first in coining this phrase. It was a failed attempt to rally Americans against the flood of Japanese cars into the marketplace. Buying American became a method to prove one's patriotism. Over time, the logic failed as the public became more aware that most every "American" manufacturer had diversified to such an extent as to only be correctly termed a multinational. Consumer self interest and product quality surpassed attempts to align patriotic feelings with economic reality. There still remains, however, a percentage of the population that steadfastly holds this belief.

3)   **"The War on Drugs"** - Billions of dollars are spent each year to address drug abuse and the dreaded outcome this aspect of modern life brings. One result of this governmental campaign is to establish a public mindset that any activity offshore is illicit in nature. There can be little doubt that illicit activity is present; the exact level, however, is very much in question and will perhaps never be known. It does seem a matter of common sense that financial markets are naturally going to be a depository for all sorts of funds, and reasonable due diligence can be the only expectation. Further, all industries have an element that is unsavory. For example, the United States savings and loan industry had numerous well-documented problems extending over many years. In addition, the US brokerage industry has had scandal after scandal that includes some of the largest names on Wall Street. Yet our perception of these industries is not clouded by over reaction. Painting all of the Caribbean, Pacific Rim and Europe with the same broad brush is simply unreasonable; billions of dollars move each day from these countries in the way of legitimate commerce.

4)   **"Media"** - Each evening, tabloid television reinforces the readily accepted fact that sensational stories sell. Exceptions become the norm within this journalistic framework. How information is presented to the public becomes more important than the particulars. Thus, the "spin" of a particular story becomes everything. Offshore business reports are rarely interesting unless someone is financially hurt. In addition, Hollywood has lent a hand cultivating a profile of illegitimacy with movies such as "The Firm", where cash was flown via private jet to the Cayman Islands for deposit, or "Wall Street", as offshore accounts were used to hide profits from insider trading. These images have cultivated a profile that holds little in the way of truth.

5)   **"Government Agencies"** - Bureaucratic agencies such as the IRS, have vested interests in restricting the access and desirability of overseas markets. Their power base could be potentially eroded if the offshore market was perceived in a more positive light and if an open-door policy was maintained for currency movement. This is reflected in the increased filings now required by the US Government for moving currency offshore. These restrictions would likely be even stronger except for potentially devastating effects on the US economy. Every government action taken within the financial markets has an equal reaction that is not always desirable. The US economy is very much dependent upon foreign investment that would not react well to stricter controls on the movement of money. This highlights the inherent struggle between the State Department, with its international interests wishing to maintain policies that avoid economic retaliatory measures by foreign governments, and the IRS, with its strict domestic view.

6)   **"Giving Away Personal Privacy"** - Governments keep secrets. They often do so under the premise of national security. It should follow that individuals would have issues, perhaps of the financial nature, that would be detrimental to their well being if known by the general public or business competitors. Personal privacy, however, has been consistently undermined over the last few decades. The primary reason has been the lack of active participation by US citizens to protect their right to privacy. Additionally, the public has become willing to sacrifice its private life because of fear. Fear of crime, drugs, gangs, terror, etc. has created an environment where the idea of privacy is a low priority. Any former resident of the Soviet Union can describe in detail how intrusive a government can become and the danger of a complacent stance. Left unchecked, it is the nature of government to push the envelope and pry into the private affairs of its citizens. "Government for the people and by the people" can easily become a lost concept. Privacy remains important, because privacy is power.

"Government's view of the economy could be summed up in a few short phrases: If it moves, tax it. If it keeps moving, regulate it. And if it stops moving, subsidize it."

- Ronald Reagan

Conclusion

The term tax haven is antiquated. Predominately, the feeling in the United States is that offshore havens are used for illegitimate reasons when the opposite is true. Each day, hundreds of billions of dollars move from country to country. The vast majority of these transactions are a reflection of the evolving world economy. Ironically, the U.S. government is not only an active participant in the offshore marketplace but in many documented instances openly endorses its use.

Chapter 3

9/11 Changes everything . . .

Most of us viewed the tragic images broadcasted on September 11, 2001 with horror, disbelief and rage. While time may have diminished the raw emotions and shock of that infamous day, 9/11 will continue to remain a definitive moment in our nation's history. Ask almost anyone and likely they can recall exactly where they were and what they were doing when our country's security landscape was forever changed.

Post 9/11, the global business environment has been changed in many profound ways. Politics and business may have never been so tightly woven together. Ripples have been felt from the securities/ banking industry to mom and pop cash businesses, even to the United Nations. Airline travel and the safety measures surrounding it have been severely altered. The United States has found itself on two war  fronts. The OECD became a political force black listing sovereign nations while the new and friendly IRS has come and gone. Additionally, The Patriot Act hurriedly came into existence.

"Tis the business of little minds to shrink; but he whose heart is firm, and whose conscience approves his conduct, will pursue his principles unto death."

- Thomas Paine

In this chapter we offer past writings that have appeared in our firm's magazine published since 1999. The purpose of this is to provide perspective. Lapse of time tends to alter memory and September 11, 2001 can never be forgotten. Our starting point is immediately following 9/11; from there we will go through a few of the more controversial business events that followed. If you choose to stay with us on this track we think you will see the relevance to offshore vehicles.

The Business of Good vs. Evil

By Jeffrey H. Corbett
Editor & Co-Publisher, C&K Magazine

www.CK-Magazine.com Published Fall 2001

It was 1986 and I was in New York for the first time. My associate and I were in "The City" on business. During the off hours, like most visitors we toured New York as much as possible. One evening at dusk we found ourselves at the foot of an impressive elevator bank where a man wearing a tuxedo greeted us. "Welcome to the Windows of the World," the gentleman said. He must have uttered those words literally thousands of times. They haunt me today. The elevator doors opened and within seconds, the two of us were catapulted 110 floors to the top of the World Trade Center.

Does God have favorites? Does he or she with all the wisdom of the universe choose one people over another? Does our place of birth which results in nationality, culture and frequently religion, doom or propel us? Do you have the right to tell me your god is better than mine? Will you die for it?

The Dark Ages, specifically the time between 500 AD - 1,000 AD was a period in human history where surprisingly little is known. Turmoil was the human condition; Rome was gone, urban life had vanished, illiteracy was everywhere, barbarian hordes warred for land – certainly not representative of a period that most in the civilized world would aspire to repeat. The Crusades followed. Starting with a speech given by Pope Urban II on November 27, 1095, approximately four hundred years ensued with Christians trying to impose their beliefs by

"Patriotism is your conviction that this country is superior to all other countries because you were born in it."

- George Bernard Shaw

21

force, on the rest of the world. The dogs of war were unleashed. A millennium of time has passed, yet how much have we learned?

In the business world, one discovers early on to avoid discussing religion and politics. Passions run so deep on these subjects that you are just as likely to offend as to endear. After September 11, 2001, the collision of values caused by religion, politics and business may never have been so intertwined. So here we sit, at the intersection of all three in this new-world or as "The Who" once lamented in a song, "new boss…same old boss."

We simply do not learn.

"Never let your sense of morals prevent you from doing what's right."

- Isaac Asimov

The difficulties we confront are not faced by one nation, people or religion but by all mankind. Like it or not we are all tied together. Like it or not we have the military might to end our existence or the beginnings of technology capable of greatness beyond our wildest dreams. Challenges abound and, in the subsequent environment, tolerance and intelligent leadership is at premium.

Yet since that terrible day in September, radical positions using visceral appeal have surfaced with their own, seemingly heartless agendas. In the midst of national tragedy, while mourning families suffered from previously unimaginable actions, others could not wait to spin their rhetoric. They demonstrated a lack of sensitivity that defies description.

A shocking case in point occurred during a September 13, 2001 broadcast of "The 700 Club" television show. The inflammatory nature of these comments verge on being unpatriotic and hate mongering. Both Jerry Falwell and Pat Robertson suggested that "pagans" and other Americans whose lifestyle and political beliefs they listed during the broadcast and differed from their own, had helped the attack happen by immoral behavior.

Many would happily see unrelated matters come into play. It is therefore, incumbent upon the silent majority in predominately Muslim, Jewish or Christian states to shout down this insanity and offer a reasonable voice or a terrible price will be paid. It will be paid with blood and in the name of religion; fanatics do not know their plight.

In this atmosphere, the offshore business world is an easy target but is it really part of the problem? A plausible answer to that question is both yes and no. Those jurisdictions that have proven to be lax in regulation of the financial markets have obviously been short-sighted and perhaps become their own worst enemy. If you want to be truly objective however, you must acknowledge that some of the largest financial scandals in history have occurred in the strict environment that is the United States. The 1991 Bank of Credit and Commerce International (BCCI) springs to mind. The logical conclusion is that regulation alone is not the answer. It is also important to note that while many countries typically referred to as tax havens have, in reality, been very cooperative with anti-money laundering legislation.

> *"Those who stand for nothing fall for anything."*
>
> *- Alexander Hamilton*

We should therefore be leery of those who wish to drag ancillary and often unrelated issues into this already complicated picture. They wish to do nothing more than promote their own frequently skewed principles. With this in mind, in the international business arena, the Organization for Economic Cooperation and Development (OECD) lurks with its "one world, one tax" mentality. The Bush Administration was quick to recognize its flaws and distanced itself from the OECD prior to September 11th. Now however it seems to be "flirting" with the OECD. We hope this is not the case.

Targeting smaller jurisdictions as the OECD has done and will do nothing except serve those looking at this as an opportunity to use pressure tactics to raise global tax rates. Terrorists do not worry about taxes.

As you may recall, the OECD was originally founded in 1961. Its predecessor was the Organization for European Economic Cooperation (OEEC) which was formed to administer American and Canadian aid under the Marshall Plan for reconstruction after World War II. Since taking over for its forerunner, the OECD has a stated objective to "build strong economies in its member countries, to improve efficiency, hone market systems, expand free trade and contribute to the development in industrialized as well as developing countries." Most recently however, this Paris based organization has looked to extend its influence far beyond traditional objectives to include non-member nations. So much has been written about the OECD and its "Harmful Tax Practices Committee" that there is little purpose in revisiting it here. Its standing order to blacklist sovereign governments because of incentives they can offer in a free marketplace seems…well, un-American. The September 11th heartbreak should not be maneuvered into a rallying point for such self-serving organizations.

Prime Minister Lester B. Bird of Antigua and Barbuda recently outlined what many feel. "The scheme has its genesis in the left-wing ideology of certain European Treasury Departments that believe in the notion of high taxation. These ideologues have caused European member nations of the OECD to be the highest taxed nations of the world. Unable to tax their population any further without running the risk of not being re-elected, they have decided to set upon companies and persons whose investments attract either low tax or no tax from foreign jurisdictions. The purpose is to force elected governments and legislatures to fix tax rates within a framework dictated by the OECD for the benefit of some OECD members."

Tax havens actually promote international commerce and freedom. They provide credible protection against one's own government becoming too powerful and the proverbial invisible bureaucrat imposing restrictive policies. Surprisingly, depending on one's perspective, almost every country represents a tax haven of some sort. For example, in the United States, foreign investors do not pay tax upon interest earned from bank Certificates of Deposit. A shift in this policy would result in large sums of money looking for investment elsewhere. Most however, would never place the US in a tax haven category.

> *"Always vote for principle, though you may vote alone, and you may cherish the sweetest reflection that your vote is never lost."*
>
> *- John Quincy Adams*

Therefore, great care should be taken before painting the subject matter with a broad stroke. The remedy is to be found in demonstrating courage and the ability to focus on the real objective. Our patriotic duty is to guard personal liberties and promote affluence through the expansion of international business and a free marketplace. Thus, through education, hope and freedom, we can drag the rest of the world into the 21st century.

The solution does not mean turning a blind eye; it is not unpatriotic to question one's government. Rather, it is incumbent upon us to hold our government accountable for its policies. We should insist that a "New Deal" foreign policy be developed that addresses the economic disparity between developed and undeveloped nations. Future policy must be more meaningful than merely handing out money; it should pave the way for significant economic relationships. We should insist upon alternative fuel sources being developed. As it stands, the United States is the world's only superpower but is tethered by an umbilical cord to the Middle East and its oil. This is simply an unacceptable weakness. Finally, many United States' Government agencies have been asleep at the switch and should be held accountable. The extent of influence demonstrated by airline lobbyist groups and their lack of regard for anything but the bottom line points to major flaws in the system. This cannot be allowed to stand. International business must be able to travel with safety and confidence. You cannot teleconference a handshake.

"Always forgive your enemies - nothing annoys them so much."

- Oscar Wilde

Absolutely none of these issues are beyond our reach; if we maintain our resolve, all can be accomplished. The single greatest tribute to those who were lost on that tragic day would be to make 9/11 a turning point in history. Let's bring opportunity and freedom to every corner of the globe. Let's do our part as the international business community and expand free markets and capitalism beyond the enemy's worst nightmares.

Dedicated to my father's good friend, his son and all those who perished September 11, 2001.

Is the US Chasing Business Offshore?

By Jeffrey H. Corbett and Patrick J. Kish, C&K Magazine

www.CK-Magazine.com Published Summer 2002

During the late 1940's and the 1950's, a climate of irrational fear flourished in the United States. A deep seeded apprehension of Communism had taken hold throughout much of the free world. As the Soviet Union developed into a nuclear superpower, this anxiety reached a fevered pitch where the politically ambitious could harvest the benefits.

"Are you now or have you ever been a Communist?" Senator Joseph McCarthy

"The most tragic paradox of our time is to be found in the failure of nation-states to recognize the imperatives of internationalism."

- Earl Warren

PSST…Is it safe to come out yet? American CEOs have been running for cover. Criminal behavior by a handful of corporate executives has harmed innocents and shaken core markets. On the other hand, at what point does the response to corruption in the corporate boardroom go past reason and reach hysteria? Can the reaction actually be counter-productive and in the long term damage the much needed economic base needed to wage war on terrorism?

The 9/11 tragedy would seem to be the facilitator of the current business crisis facing the United States. In truth, however, the house has been out of order for some time. Prior to 9/11, conflicting political and economic foes were facing-off for an important and historic encounter. At stake were the future of a domestic tax collection agency and the direction of international business. The climate was one of a much-contested presidential election and a stock market bubble waiting to burst.

The House Out of Order

Domestically, the Internal Revenue Service was under fire. Citizens had filed complaints, which had largely been ignored by legislators for decades. The depth of taxpayer bitterness towards the IRS however, had been buried until numerous well-documented cases began to surface. In September of 1997, the Senate Finance Committee held three days of hearings to review IRS practices and procedures. More than 1,000 tax-payers had been contacted who claimed mistreatment.

"Our six month long look at the IRS shows a troubled agency with widespread, serious problems. At a minimum, the cases brought to our attention, paint a picture of an unresponsive agency with some employees who do not care about the taxpayers they serve. At worst, our investigation has uncovered an agency in which a subculture of fear and intimidation has been allowed to flourish – both in the internal treatment of some employees and in the treatment of some taxpayers."
Chairman William V. Roth Jr. (R-DE)

Change would be hard, if not impossible. The complexity and ambiguity of the United States tax code compounded with how its enforcement arm treated taxpayers had created a huge cottage industry. Professionals by the score developed a vested interest in maintaining the status quo that enabled them to peddle their wares as tax reduction specialists.

Mixed Signals

Internationally, the United States was sending mixed messages. First, it had entertained the idea of backing the effort focusing on tax harmonization by the Organization for Economic Cooperation and Development (OECD). The OECD was in the midst of finalizing its blacklist for what it had termed,

"The attempt to combine wisdom and power has only rarely been successful and then only for a short while."

- Albert Einstein

"uncooperative tax havens" which they defined as those countries that did not adhere to the OECD's principles of transparency and effective exchange of information. The OECD launched this initiative in a report published in April 1998, setting criteria for identifying such tax havens and for actions that could be implemented against them. It was only after the Bush Administration took office that Treasury Secretary Paul O'Neil changed policy direction by flatly stating that the US would not back such efforts.

"Power tends to corrupt and absolute power corrupts absolutely."

- Lord Acton

At the same time, the United Sates was busy protecting its own $4 billion a year tax break program, entitled Foreign Sales Corporations or FISKS. This legal loophole enabled US exporters such as Microsoft and Boeing, to benefit from establishing an offshore entity, and through various accounting measures, obtain substantial tax breaks.

In recent years, the European Union had taken umbrage and claimed the FISK program accounted to an unfair tax scheme that violated standing agreements. As such, a complaint was filed with the World Trade Organization (WTO) resulting in ruling after ruling against the US. In essence, the United States has attempted to have it both ways.

The Current Problem

With this as the historical backdrop, some legislators are now attempting to equate patriotism with corporate taxes. The logic seems flawed in a system that promotes not only FISKS but steadfastly fights tax reform and allows states like Delaware to become, in effect, domestic tax havens. It does however, make perfect sense if one considers the political reward to be had by using a broad stroke to paint all executives in the same way and play to the rank and file. Much like McCarthyism, portraying American CEOs who consider international alternatives as "un-American" grabs headlines and easy gain. The long-term economic ramifications of such actions are yet to be determined but could be devastating.

Japan

History is a great teacher. It never pays to overestimate one's strength. In the 1980s, Japan was the rage, international business simply had to be a part of that marketplace. Even seasoned investors however, had no idea the economy of Japan was a bubble, fueled by a room and ready to burst by the 1990's. Japan's rise was shattered by the collapse of the Tokyo stock market and a banking system burdened with bad loans. What followed was a mass corporate exodus leaving a country that ten years later still struggles to digest its economic turn-around. Eerie parallel exists.

The Japanese had over-estimated the health of their economy. In effect, they believed that no matter their domestic course, international investment would follow. Ignoring history by being arrogant and chastising business for the actions of a few could be a dangerous path for US legislators.

Corporate Reaction

Business expatriation is not new and is most frequently a corporate reaction to economic policy or over-regulation. In the case of the United States and the alleged wave of publicly held companies inverting or going offshore – burdensome tax policy is the likely culprit. In response, legislators have two choices. (1) New restrictions on commerce could be implemented to chase after tax dollars which have, in essence been tagged "accounts receivable." (2) Innovative avenues could be opened to entice business to stay and also bring in new business. Thus resulting in a bigger economic base to draw upon.

Hidden Agendas

A rash of political and economic maneuvering has occurred since September of last year. Much of the effort has dealt with national security. Many issues are merely special interest programs from both sides of the political isle attempting to sneak under the radar screen, or simply politicians playing to the crowd.

Consider the following:

The IRS: It may in fact be stronger than ever. A very troubled agency a year ago, little has been done in the way of establishing meaningful oversight to protect taxpayer's rights. New policies have in fact significantly raised the amount of random audits to be conducted this year.

Noteworthy Attacks on Inversion

1. Connecticut's Attorney General recently sided with labor and aggressively went after Stanley Works, a 159 year old resident of New Britain, Connecticut for considering a move to Bermuda.

2. California's State Treasurer black listed public companies that moved offshore from the investment in that state's huge pension fund.

3. President George W. Bush stated, "I think American Companies ought to pay taxes and be good citizens." The President apparently is willing to ignore any potential previous involvement by his Vice President or himself as corporate board members in offshore matters.

Imperialism

The agenda put forth by the OECD to blacklist targeted small jurisdictions for unfair tax practices seems to violate the sovereignty of independent nations. Additionally, such a policy is hard to justify while attempting to promote a free marketplace.

Reason and Clarity

Before we Americans throw the "baby out with the bath water" perhaps it would be wise for us to take a collective deep breath. Certainly, recent business scandals emanating from publicly traded companies are inexcusable. The final toll in lost jobs and worthless stock will be almost incalculable. White-collar crime, long a joke, should be prosecuted to the full extent of the law.

Hidden agendas are real and virtually lurk around every corner. Politicians jump on public sentiment as fast as network television runs to the scene of a tragedy. Prosecutors, who are willing to attack business just to further their own careers, are not doing the public a service.

"If we were going to be absolutely safe we'd have to restrict people's freedoms to the point that it wouldn't be America anymore."

- Representative Frank D. Lucas
(R - Oklahoma)

We would suggest that in this time of war, business is vital to the security of the United States. It should be courted and not flogged like the proverbial red-headed stepchild. Demonizing companies like Stanley Works for trying to remain competitive in the international market makes for good headline and might currently play well with the masses but, in the long run will cost jobs.

Complicated and burdensome US tax law is the cause for corporate relocations. The general trend is towards globalization in business, which points to exactly how antiquated US tax legislation has become. As usual, politicians are ducking the real issue which is tax reform. This not only results in lost taxable income but chases future industry prospects away. What entrepreneur in their "right mind" would want to come to the United States if this type of environment is allowed to prevail?

Business Commentary
FBI Oversight: Better Late Than Never

By Patrick J. Kish
Co-Publisher, C&K Magazine

www.CK-Magazine.com Published Spring 2007

As the old adage goes, "Give them an inch, and they'll take a mile."

Over the past few weeks, Congress has been in uproar over the discovery that the FBI systematically abused and violated our privacy using authorities granted by the Patriot Act. The vague laws were hastily enacted in the wake of the September 11th attacks, allowing for this infringement of our rights.

A report by the Justice Department's Inspector General, Glenn Fine, found that 48 violations of law or presidential directive were committed by the FBI and that a significant number of violations had not been identified or reported. The report also states that the FBI substantially underreported to Congress the amount of National Security Letters issued regarding U.S. citizens, a letter that can be used to acquire email, telephone, travel and financial records including credit and bank transactions. Fine believes the FBI underreported the amount of letters by at least 17%.

Commerce in the age of technology is different than years before. Today, most business is conducted electronically, and even with all of the safeguards that businesses, financial institutions and retailers make, a criminal can purchase your credit card information for $1.00 and purchase your entire identity for $14.00. Financial privacy is at an all time low. This revelation and the newest breach of personal privacy makes it very clear that even if you do not fit a terrorist profile,

"The insult is to call this a 'patriot bill'... I thought it was undermining the Constitution, so I didn't vote for it — and therefore I'm somehow not a patriot. That's insulting."

- Representative Ron Paul (R - Texas)

your identity is at risk. Even more so, without any credible government oversight.

"This is a serious breach of trust" said Rep. John Conyers, Democrat of Michigan, chairman of the U.S. Judiciary Committee.

"Our whole constitutional heritage rebels at the thought of giving government the power to control men's minds."

- Thurgood Marshall

Now, Congress is scurrying to determine whether the Patriot Act has allowed the FBI to reach too far into the lives of Americans, with some senators and representatives calling for a revision of the Patriot Act. Arlen Specter, a Republican Senator from Pennsylvania has said congress may have to "change the law to impose statutory requirements and perhaps take away some of the authority which we've already given to the FBI, since they appear not to be able to know how to use it." Others including John Sununu, a Republican senator from New Hampshire, are calling for the replacement of Attorney General Alberto Gonzales.

There is no doubt that we are living in a time when personal privacy rights are being trampled. Even worse, is the fact that the perpetrators at the center of this mess are the appointed officials at the Justice Department and the Federal Bureau of Investigation; the very same people hired to advocate and protect the security of U.S. Citizens.

Conclusion

September 11, 2001 remains one of the most tragic events in our country's modern history changing not only the fundamental security landscape in the U.S. but also daily patterns of life, the international business environment and citizen's overall sense of Patriotism and allegiance to this nation. While we in no way seek to lessen the terror and emotions associated with these attacks, we do feel it necessary to shed light onto the many changes that have taken place in our post 9/11 world.

Following September 11th, many new governmental agencies were created including:

• *The Department of Homeland Security*

"Formed in November 2002 to "develop and coordinate the implementation of a comprehensive national strategy to secure the United States from terrorist threats or attacks. The Office will coordinate the executive branch's efforts to detect, prepare for, prevent, protect against, respond to, and recover from terrorist attacks within the United States."

• *The Information Awareness Office*
(Amended to "Terrorist Information Awareness" in May 2003)

"Formed in January 2002 with the aim of developing technology that would enable it to collect and process massive amounts of information about every individual in the United States, and trace patterns of behavior that could help predict terrorist activities. The information the IAO would gather includes Internet activity, credit card purchase histories, airline ticket purchases, car rentals, medical records, educational transcripts, driver's licenses, utility bills, tax returns, and other available data."

- *9/11 Commission*

"Formed in November 2002 to "to prepare a full and complete account of the circumstances surrounding the September 11, 2001 attacks", including preparedness for and the immediate response to the attacks. The commission was also mandated to provide recommendations designed to guard against future attacks."

"There is nothing wrong with America that cannot be cured with what is right in America."

- William J. Clinton

While all three of the above agencies were created initially to protect America and its citizens from potential, future attacks, these agencies have been under consistent criticism for "over-stepping" their bounds. American citizens, recognize it or not, have lost many of their personal privacy rights under the guise of "national security." Most notably, with the inception of the **Patriot Act**, law enforcement agencies were given more authority to search the phone, email and financial records of some citizens while wiretaps and searches of suspected homes and businesses were made more accessible. International security measures that have inhibited the civil liberties of citizens include hidden cameras & microphones in public transportation areas like taxis and subway stations as well as roving taps, illegal search & seizures and more.

Additionally, patterns of daily life were altered in the aftermath of these events; from obvious changes like increased security measures that came with the creation of the Transportation Security Administration (TSA), to censorship in the radio and film industry. When reminded of these discrepancies before and after the attacks, it provides for an interesting perspective.

• Prior to the creation of the TSA, private companies were contracted with individual airports or airlines to handle security screenings. Come 2001, all screening equipment and companies used must be approved by the TSA. Since its inception, the TSA has regulated products that cannot be carried on airplanes such as knifes and razor blades, and has mandated the way in which liquids and gels must be transported.

• In the wake of 9/11, Clear Channel Communications, which owns over 1,200 radio stations distributed a list of songs they deemed "lyrically questionable" to play after the attacks. While these songs were not outright banned, radio stations were heavily discouraged from playing them on air. Some of the 166 songs on the list included, all songs by the band Rage against the Machine, "Knocking on Heaven's Door" by Bob Dylan and even the Bangles' hit "Walk like an Egyptian."

• Hollywood took precautions in the post 9/11 world by altering, cancelling or delaying films that unintentionally evoked the disaster. Films and television shows that took place in New York removed images of the World Trade Center in scenes and in their credits. Additionally any plot lines with references to terrorism were immediately changed and/or delayed.

Changes in the global business marketplace have resulted in unintended, positive changes in the offshore world since the events of September 11, 2001. New restrictions have been implemented across jurisdictional borders that have greatly increased the reputation and prestige of conducting business internationally.

• Offshore Banking accounts are now much harder to open than in previous years.

• Funds in these accounts must be sourced.

• Bank Licenses are harder to obtain and the paid in capital requirements to open accounts has been raised significantly.

• Information sharing agreements between countries has made the offshore industry's reputation more positive overall.

It is our hope that by republishing some of our magazine's past articles, we were able to provide this important perspective into changes in the global business environment resulting from this infamous event. As you can see from these various works, the changes that took place directly affected the offshore marketplace and ultimately provide the framework for the following chapter that outlines why you should go offshore now.

Chapter 4

Why Go Offshore... Not for tax purposes.

Everyone wants tax benefits; but, if you are a U.S. citizen, it's simply not that easy. Until the early 1960's and the Kennedy Administration, obtaining tax benefits was merely a matter of moving your assets offshore. With the advent of worldwide income tax, you must now be aware of tax law and various IRS rulings related to this subject. Additionally, a great deal of negative and inaccurate information has been written on this topic which is why it is essential to educate yourself. As always, we strongly suggest the use of a good international business and tax attorney.

The United States has a long history of tax revolt; it joins the rest of the world in the desire to "avoid the tax man". Macroeconomics is steeped in tax theory. Professor of Business Economics at the University of Southern California, Arthur Laffer is credited with first authoring a concept now known as the "Laffer Curve". Its premise is that taxation will produce the same amount of revenue for government coffers at a low percentage as it will at a much higher percentage. There are many reasons for this, none of which include a reduction in work force motivation and/or residents looking to alternative methods of shelter. In our case this could include the use of offshore vehicles.

"In politics stupidity is not a handicap."

- Napoleon

This phenomenon is a well-known economic theory and certainly seems to reflect the essence of true human behavior. As Dr. Laffer noted, "there are always two tax rates that yield the same revenues". When an aide for then President Gerald Ford asked him to elaborate, Laffer drew a simple curve with powerful implications. He further explained, "When the tax rate is 100 percent, all production ceases in the money economy. People will not work if the fruits of their labors are confiscated by the government. Thus, government revenues fall to zero. On the other hand, if the tax rate is zero, people can keep 100 percent of what they produce. Production is maximized. But because the tax rate is zero, the government revenues are again zero. In between lies the curve. At some point along that curve is the point where tax revenues and production are maximized."[1]

Figure 1 is a graphic illustration of the concept of the Laffer Curve--not the exact levels of taxation corresponding to specific levels of revenues. At a tax rate of 0 percent, the government would collect no tax revenues, no matter how large the tax base. Likewise, at a tax rate of 100 percent, the government would also collect no tax revenues because no one would willingly work for an after-tax wage of zero (i.e., there would be no tax base). Between these two extremes there are two tax rates that will collect the same amount of revenue: a high tax rate on a small tax base and a low tax rate on a large tax base.

The Laffer Curve

Supply-side economic theory, similar to the Laffer Curve, popular during the Reagan years, has its detractors. George H.W. Bush for example, labeled such theory, "Voodoo Economics." Politicians rarely have embraced such a position. A seemingly time-honored cure for governments

---

[1] Jude Wanniski, The Wall Street Journal, June 1978

that find revenues falling is to dramatically increase the number and authority of tax collectors. This technique, often favored by modern governments, is predestined to further reduce the revenue flow to the treasury.

Adam Smith, author of <u>The Wealth of Nations</u>, a classic economic work, made his position clear pertaining to this issue. "Every tax ought to be so contrived as to both take out and keep out of the pockets of the people as little as possible, over and above what it brings to the public treasury of the state." He further goes on to give four reasons why the State should avoid this folly.

First, the levying of it may require a greater number of officers, those whose salaries may eat up a larger part of the produce of the tax and whose prerequisites may impose another additional tax upon the people.

"The constitution only gives people the right to pursue happiness. You have to catch it yourself."
- Ben Franklin

Secondly, it may obstruct the industry of the people and discourage them from applying to certain branches of business which might give maintenance and employment to great multitudes. While it obliges the people to pay, it may thus diminish, or perhaps destroy, some of the funds which might enable them to do so.

Thirdly, by forfeitures and other penalties which these unfortunate individuals incur, those who attempt unsuccessfully to evade the tax, it may frequently ruin them, and thereby put an end to the benefit which the community might have received from the employment of their capitals. An injudicious tax offers a great temptation to smuggling, but the penalties of smuggling must rise in proportion to the temptation. The law, contrary to all ordinary principles of justice, first creates the temptation then punishes those who yield to it. It commonly enhances the punishment in proportion to the very circumstances which ought certainly to alleviate it, the temptation to commit the crime.

Fourth, by subjecting the people to frequent visit and odious examination of the tax-gatherers, it may expose them to unnecessary trouble, vexation and oppression. Although vexation is not expense, strictly speaking, it is certainly equivalent to the expense at which every man would be willing to redeem himself from it.

The abuse by tax collectors Smith spoke of is historic fact. Concepts of income tax have been changing in the United States, as elsewhere, for hundreds of years. "President Lincoln established the Bureau of Internal Revenue in 1862, the direct predecessor of today's IRS. Originally, those considered wealthy, with incomes above $10,000 were taxed at a 5% rate while 3% was the standard for incomes above $600. Individuals earning under $600 a year were exempt. Tax collectors were paid a commission of 4% on all money collected up to $100,000 and 2% above that level." This lead to widespread abuse and corruption. By 1863, the Bureau of Internal Revenue was firmly entrenched as a strong arm of the Central American government, employing an army of four thousand. Only three years later, however, Congress appointed a Special Revenue Commission charged with reforming the scandal-ridden bureau. In 1872, the income tax was repealed.[2]

---

[2] Shelley L. Davis, "Unbridled Power" p.190

Politicians and the public have long struggled with the idea of income tax and what is a fair amount to pay the government to maintain services. Income tax in the United States would not reappear in earnest until the early twentieth century. "Income tax was seen as being the most efficient means to keep capitalists and monopolists from amassing huge fortunes. Theodore Roosevelt denounced such wealth in 1906 as fortunes swollen beyond all healthy limits."[3]

Prior to that, the United States Supreme Court issued a very noteworthy ruling in 1895. The court ruled on a suit brought about by wealthy tax protesters; their claim was that income tax was unconstitutional, as it was not proportioned among all citizens. In other words, a direct tax on the people would have to be equal.

This political positioning went back and forth until October 3, 1913, when President Woodrow Wilson signed into law the first personal income tax since the Civil War. Our current income tax can be directly traced to this legislation. Surprisingly however, the tax law passed at that time was only fourteen pages long, in comparison to the almost incomprehensible code that stands today.

---

[3] Ibid., p.192

With the evolution of tax, methods to shelter income have also metamorphosed. According to the renowned international accounting firm of Arthur Andersen & Co., the emotions of a tax shelter can be understood within the following context, "The term tax shelter often elicits a strong reaction from those who encounter it. To some, a tax shelter is a giveaway device designed to enrich the high-bracket taxpayer at the expense of the "average" taxpayer. It is a gimmick, a loophole, a proof of Mr. Bumble's assertion that ". . . the law is an ass. . ." In reality and in fairness, a tax shelter is neither of these. A tax shelter is nothing more than an investment structured to yield the maximum tax benefit from certain provisions incorporated into tax law achieve specific purposes. Whether those purposes encourage specific types of investment, to achieve a social goal or cater to the demands of so-called "special interests" is irrelevant to the investment decision. The incentives are there to be used. They are based on law and are not meant to be measured against standards of fairness or morality. [4] *

As recently as the 1980's, an ample number of shelters were readily available. Some of these would include tax write-offs of 2-1, 3-1 and possibly greater. The rule of thumb was the greater the write off, the more risk involved in the investment and the higher the potential for IRS scrutiny. The greatest number of possibilities revolved around limited partnerships structured for oil drilling and real estate industries. Other industries that offered possible incentives included: equipment leasing, farming, timber and motion pictures. The Authors of this work can remember well, while working as brokers, being flown to Odessa, Texas, for the promotion of one oil and gas partnership. This was common practice. Limited partnerships, however, had most of their tax incentives eliminated with the tax law change that occurred in 1986.

---

[4] Arthur Andersen & Co., "Tax Shelters - The Basics" p.4

* *Arthur Andersen & Co based in Chicago, was once one of the "Big 5" accounting firms however in 2002, the firm voluntarily surrendered its licenses after being found guilty to charges relating to Enron. The Supreme Court overturned the verdict and restored their license.*

It becomes apparent, therefore, that income tax and potential shelters are dynamic concepts. They change with the time, national origin and surrounding economic climate. Since these suppositions do not remain stagnate, logic would dictate that neither can our understanding. Many variables come into play when considering offshore vehicles for shelter. We would suggest the following:

1. We will reiterate that no part of this publication is meant to provide tax advice. You should consult a good international business and tax attorney. This is an imperative measure, no matter your country of origin.

2. Considering our experience, having consulted thousands of individuals on the establishment of offshore structures, it is very seldom a good idea to use an international vehicle exclusively for tax reasons. Similar in nature to the use of limited partnerships in the 1980's, the structure should be reviewed first for quality. One considerable exception would have been the establishment of a Foreign Sales Corporation for a U.S. manufacturer, yet these entities no longer exist.

3. U.S. investors should be aware of the following IRS rulings as defined:

a. **CFC or Controlled Foreign Corporation Tax**

Prior to 1962, it was legal for U.S. persons to form foreign corporations to hold investment assets and to not owe any U.S. tax on the investment income until the income was repatriated to the U.S. Congress became concerned that using foreign corporations to avoid U.S. taxes was becoming much too popular. They changed the tax law so that taxes would be imposed on certain U.S. owners of foreign corporations to the extent of any passive investment income received by the foreign corporation.

b. FPHC or Foreign Personal Holding Corporation Tax

A penalty tax imposed on corporations that accumulate predominately investment-type income (other than capital gains). This tax was created to prevent an individual from transferring dividend-paying investments to a corporation and then using the dividend received deduction to avoid taxable income.

c. Accumulated Earnings Tax

Created to prevent corporations from avoiding income tax at the shareholder level by accumulating rather than distributing excess earnings and profit. The AET is a 15% penalty tax imposed on corporations that accumulate earnings and profits above and beyond reasonable business needs. Excluded corporations include, personal holding companies, passive foreign investment companies and tax-exempt organizations.

"Privacy is essential not only to the souls of painters and poets, who thrive in solitude, but to the rest of us too-individuals whose canvas is our lives."
– Sue Halpern

d. Foreign Source Income

Taxable income from sources outside the United States that can include but is not limited to, interest, dividends, compensation for personal services, rents and royalties, and net income from the sale of property. "Foreign source income" is gross income, less expenses, losses, and other deductions properly apportioned or allocated thereto and a ratable part of any other expenses, losses, or deductions that cannot be allocated to some item or class of gross income.

Chapter 5

Why Go Offshore NOW, a Macro View

Now that we have dispelled some of the popular misconceptions for "going offshore", this chapter presents the most prominent benefits that can be attained legally & ethically. Profit, Privacy and Asset Protection make up a few of the common reasons business professionals, investors and entrepreneurs all seek ownership of private financial institutions offshore.

Profit

Perhaps no benefit afforded to individuals who decide to "go offshore" is as important as increasing profit. The two main methods of making a profit are by cutting costs and selling more. The concept of going offshore for profit is based in a common principle: less regulation results in lower overhead and higher profit margins. This can apply to numerous industries including banking, insurance, manufacturing, shipping and trading, just to name a few.

For many years now, the concept of "offshore outsourcing" has been the front runner in the quest for increased profit. By definition, "offshoring" is the process of relocating business processes from one country to another. This may include production, manufacturing and/or services. Most simply, the economic logic behind offshoring lies in the ability to obtain the same goods and services for less cost than in the home country.

The two basic types of offshore outsourcing are information technology and business processes. Information technology refers to computer programming, data analysis, and transcription, while business processes can include call centers and claims processing. Based on the type of offshoring services desired, there are many countries to consider yet, for the most part, the main player involved include India, China, Brazil, and the Philippines, to name a few.

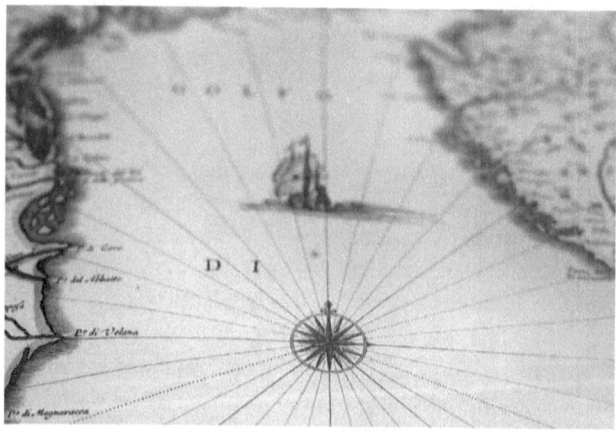

In order for an individual and their business endeavors to continue to profit and expand, they must be able to sell more products and services. Additionally, the need to provide clients with new services on a continuous basis further increases production and ultimately profit. Owning an offshore private institution enables businesses to expand by offering new services, of which they were previously not capable, to gain membership to prestigious international financial processing systems, to move money and investments at a quicker rate to capitalize on new opportunities and much more.

Privacy

In addition to profit, the benefit of increased privacy is one the main motivations for going offshore. The advances of modern society have caused our lives to move at a faster pace than in previous years, mostly due to the computer age and the instant access to information it offers. For many, this may be not only disheartening but precarious. Wealth, fame and business success are just a few factors that can make an individual a target for unwarranted probes by those that are less than scrupulous. The average person must also contend with the potential problem of information theft. Serious damage to one's records or finances can result. Disclosures of private information, for reasons other than what was originally intended, have become a consequence of the times in which we live.

"Never doubt that a small group of thoughtful committed citizens can change the world. Indeed, it's the only thing that ever has."

- Margaret Mead

"Banks and other institutions readily proclaim that their policy is one of strict confidentiality yet in reality can be quite different. For example, in the 1970's, the White House "plumbers" discovered that Daniel Ellisberg had been seeing a psychiatrist; knowledge found by prying into his bank records. With that information, the secret Nixon administration investigative unit was able to plan the break-in into the psychiatrist's office in search of records."[1]

Even if you find personal privacy to be a luxury, consider your Social Security Number. "Social Security cards are used for identity checks; it is absurdly unreliable. This means that with this number someone can probably obtain military information, bank information, college grades, etc."[2] In other words, the potential for fraud becomes very real. Thus, identity theft has become a more common crime.

[1] Robert Ellis Smith "Privacy: How to Protect What's Left of It" p. 15
[2] Ibid. p.159

It is interesting to note that Social Security numbers were not originally intended to be used as that type of tool. They have evolved into a convenient national identification card. Social Security numbers were first introduced by the Social Security Act of 1935. The initial purpose was strictly for the social security program. In 1943, President Roosevelt signed Executive Order 9397, requiring federal agencies to use the number when creating new record-keeping systems. That was followed by the IRS adoption of the number as a taxpayer ID in 1961. The Tax Reform Act of 1976 enabled state and local tax, welfare, driver's license, or motor vehicle registration authorities to use this number to establish identities. The dilemma is that many organizations, in addition to the previously mentioned government agencies, now accept these numbers as authentication of identification.

"Suing for damages has become both a huge industry and a tremendous drag on American industry's ability to compete."
- Forbes Magazine

The dehumanizing effects of national identification cards, such as the Social Security card, and the potential for governmental abuse have become the concern of several human rights groups. One such organization is Privacy International, formed in 1990 as a watchdog. Based in London, it claims members in more than forty countries and follows issues pertaining to surveillance by governments and corporations. Their stated intent is to raise awareness about the dangers of national ID card systems, military surveillance, medical records, data matching, telephone tapping, police information systems and credit reporting.

According to Privacy International many countries are actively considering adopting national ID cards for a variety of functions. This would include the United States, the United Kingdom, Canada, Australia, New Zealand, the Philippines and Thailand.

Privacy, however, is not just a political or ideological matter; it has tremendous meaning in everyday life. Any corporate manager that has ever e-mailed an employee can attest to this need. Trade secrets, client lists, portfolio information, potential business ventures are just a few examples that require privacy for business success.

Cyberspace now represents the newest battleground for privacy. As recently as a decade ago, the United States government was involved in a battle for cyber privacy. Philip R. Zimmermann created a computer encryption program called "pretty good privacy", or "PGP." Mr. Zimmermann wrote his program with human rights in mind and gave it away for free on the Internet in 1991. The federal government proceeded with a criminal investigation, claiming that he had violated Arms trafficking laws, stating the software qualified as "munitions." The government eventually dropped the case. We would suggest that those interested in exploring this story in more detail check out the multitude of sources available on the internet.

The government's classification of the encryption software as munitions, clearly exemplifies the weight of this issue; the topic of privacy on the Internet is as important as gun control in the mind of the Federal Government.

Additionally, as we mentioned a few chapters back, the terrorist attacks of September 11, 2001 have altered American citizens' personal privacy rights. The 9/11 Commission, the Department of Homeland Security and the Information Awareness Office were all created with the intent to protect our country from potential future attacks; yet, unfortunately, many of these agencies have been criticized for over-stepping their bounds ultimately resulting in the loss of many personal privacy rights. Going offshore enables owners and investors to attain a higher degree of privacy and anonymity in their financial endeavors, much more so than in the United States.

Asset Protection

Reaching epidemic proportions, statistics now show that US citizens have a one in four chance of being sued during their lifetime. Business owners and professionals are among the most likely to be sued. Also included in that union are physicians, plastic surgeons, stockbrokers, law enforcement officials and real estate developers. Governing rules of civil procedures have been liberalized, consequentially making the process of taking legal action much easier than ever before. Results can be devastating, and products such as liability insurance are rarely enough to cover all eventualities. As a result, the use of offshore vehicles has been brought to the forefront of estate and financial planning.

An article in Forbes Magazine shed light onto this topic making the claim that "litigation is actually a much greater threat to American wealth than taxes". According to Forbes, this is due to American citizens being exposed to an infinite amount of liability through an overworked system of litigation. Thus, high-net worth individuals are putting "unlimited assets" at risk. The article goes on to state that "contrary to the popular vision of offshore banking, the true purpose of these accounts for many wealthy clients is to protect a lifetime of earnings and savings not from being taxed, but from being wiped out in a major lawsuit--say, a medical malpractice or a class-action securities litigation against an executive."

"Plastic surgeons are being named in numerous lawsuits. One Texas malpractice insurer states that current premiums are running between US $20,000-80,000 and will likely jump 20% again."
- The Economist

Since traditional estate planning procedures are no longer effective in today's "sue happy" society, the use of offshore vehicles offers potential victims a two fold strategy in its ability to (1) lower your financial profile and (2) protect your funds in such a way as to make them inaccessible.

If you are not perceived as offering deep pockets, the likelihood of legal action being taken against you is reduced. An astute person realizes that by lowering your financial profile, aggressive lawyers who get compensated on a percentage of the client's recovery, will be less likely to target you. In the rare event a plaintiff should wish to follow you offshore, they may find it a very expensive and distasteful experience. If your assets have been legally transferred overseas, and ownership of the offshore entity has been structured to capitalize upon asset protection benefits of the jurisdiction of choice, you have tipped the scales in your favor.

It is important to note that any technique employed should be set in motion years prior to a lawsuit problem. In that way, you reduce the chances of something called a "fraudulent transfer" unraveling everything. U.S. courts do not look well upon someone attempting to manipulate the legal system to avoid legitimate claims.

Aside from lowering the threat of frivolous lawsuits, another example of utilizing offshore markets to obtain a higher degree of asset protection is the 2008 Banking Crisis. Described by many as the "worst financial crisis since the Great Depression," the economic turmoil resulted in bankruptcies, mergers and foreclosures of some of the once "most premier" names on Wall Street, in addition to sending shockwaves, felt throughout the global markets.

One of the main lessons to be learned from the recent financial instability in the US markets is the need for diversification of one's investments in both domestic and offshore markets. Diversification of one's investment portfolio ensures that, should an event similar to the 2008

Banking Crisis occur again, as the saying goes, "not all of your eggs are in one basket." Additionally, the need for individuals to have more control over their funds that cannot be obtained by investing in large banks further affirms the need to look offshore at private bank ownership. For many years, large Wall Street investment banks were seen as invincible yet as unfortunate events have shown, this is indeed not the case. Individuals must protect and preserve their assets now more than ever, while at the same time enforcing their say and control over the movement and placement of those assets.

Political Concerns

In addition to the three major motivations of profit, privacy and asset protection as outlined in this chapter, there is one further reason that some individuals may seek the transitional move offshore. Unfortunately, citizens in some parts of our world face a deep concern over their nation's current political environment or policy. This holds true throughout history, across borders and whether dealing with issues of financial or personal liberties. Examples of citizens attempting to circumvent or avoid government intrusions are too plentiful to site. Omnipresent bureaucratic agencies, answering to few, inherently drive people to seek refuge. Museums have been erected to celebrate those that seek freedom. "Check Point Charlie", originally established on the border of East and West Germany, offers a dramatic example. If you have the opportunity to visit such a monument, it will likely leave a life long impression, as it did for us. The examples of those so desperate to seek freedom that risking their lives became an acceptable alternative were truly chilling. We remember looking over the Berlin Wall and recalling the words of President Kennedy "Ich bin ein Berliner"; that very carefully crafted and measured phrase spoke volumes for all people.

"The fear of possible lawsuits has changed the culture of America, an unreliability of justice is causing meltdowns in our country's common institutions and citizens no longer feel free to do what they know is right."
- USA Today

Tyrannical behavior, whether real or perceived, comes in varying degrees. Political motivation to hold assets offshore is usually based in apprehension or fear. The Iron Curtain, the Nazis of World War II, human rights violations in China, Cuba under the Castro regime, the fall of Vietnam are all at the far end of the spectrum. People however, will make a move offshore for far less. Hong Kong offers a clear and recent example of this type of political flight. The mere perception that mainland China would institute strict controls resulted in huge sums of money leaving and the migration of thousands of people.

In the United States, the well-documented abuse of power by the IRS has resulted in a move offshore by many US citizens. Both legal and illegal methods have been used to seek perceived political freedom. For many, these are not tax but civil rights issues.

"America did not invent human rights. In a very real sense, human rights invented America."
- Jimmy Carter (1981)

In his book, "A Law unto Itself, The IRS and the Abuse of Power", David Burnham provides an interesting argument. "Two hundred years ago, Madison, Jefferson, Washington and a few other clever men sat down in Philadelphia and devised a set of ethical rules to guide the new government in the conduct of its business. Congress was to pass no laws concerning the establishment of religion or the control of the press. Executive branch agencies were to make no searches of a citizen's house unless they had good reason to believe a crime had been committed and a judge further issued a warrant. The courts were required to bring the accused to trial promptly. Congress and the courts were given general supervisory authority over the executive branch. Specifically, in regard to taxation, all tax laws must originate in the House of Representatives, then viewed as the branch closest to the voters. Because of absolute demand for federal revenue, Congress and the courts have chosen to exempt the IRS from many of these checks and balances. This means that in a large proportion of tax cases, the IRS serves as policeman, prosecutor, judge, and executioner, all at the same time. The conflicts of interest inherent in this arrangement are extreme."

An investigation by Newsweek Magazine indicates further problems. "Nationwide, IRS abuses are the product of a badly dysfunctional agency, a seemingly totalitarian financial regime where bullying personalities can find a place to exercise unbridled power over people's lives. As tearful witnesses testified to the Senate, that power, wielded arbitrarily, has destroyed businesses and broken up families. In other cases, taxpayers have been unjustly imprisoned and even driven to suicide. How could this happen in America? For decades, IRS agents have had wide, almost astonishing powers to enforce the tax code; unlike any other law-enforcement officers, they have free hand to peer into and lay claim to bank accounts, pursue debt even after bankruptcy and to decide, somewhat whimsically, whether you get to keep your home or not - all without going through the courts. These powers were mostly held in check by congressional oversight and the IRS' own ridge code of ethics. But since the 1970s, a post-Watergate law ironically passed to protect taxpayers' privacy, has allowed the agency to shield itself from many inquiries into its activities. When the IRS came under pressure from Congress to show more efficiency, the agency poured its' energies into boosting seizures and case closures; top IRS managers were almost never held accountable for how they achieved these goals. And that was a recipe for abuse."[3]

The use of muscle by the IRS has driven otherwise law abiding citizens to search for extraordinary methods of protection. Again, perception is often reality. Whether or not the majority of these cases of abuse are entirely factual has little bearing on the outcome. The perception of unlawful search and seizure is sufficient to press a percentage of the population to look offshore. It is safe to assume that the percentage of disenchanted will grow with the reports of injustice.

Conclusion

There are many reasons to look offshore; most commonly are profit, privacy and asset protection. In some parts of the world, individuals seek the move offshore due to political instability and concerns. Perhaps there is no better time than now to look offshore to accomplish these essential benefits. Additionally, diversification, membership into the global marketplace and correspondent banking relationships can also be obtained and can thus further an individual's business and/or personal goals. As always, a good international business and tax attorney is highly suggested.

---

[3] Michael Hirsh, "IRS abuse of power" Newsweek Magazine

Chapter 6

"An Overview of International Financial Centers"

There is an abundance of nations, both small and large, willing to compete for your business. In certain locales in years past, after a meeting with a financial advisor, you might have sipped a daiquiri while sitting on a tropical beach. In others, you might meet a concierge and taken through plush corridors to keep an appointment with your banker. Whether your style is elegant or relaxed, international financial centers (IFC's) cater to many different cultures and preferences. In fact, for many nations the U.S. itself is an international financial haven. Personal preference aside, there are a few primary considerations that should go into any decision of jurisdiction: currency, tax treaties, and international prestige.

As all IFC's are, in most respects, foreign to the primary investor, a basic comprehension of currency transfer is a principal concern. Today, currency is transferred through data carrier systems. The Society for Worldwide Interbank Financial Telecommunications (SWIFT), based in Brussels, is the most commonly known system of transferring currency from one form to another. Through the advantages of modern technology, "hundreds of billions every day are instantaneously transferred replacing what used to require cabled instructions and confirmations."[1] While SWIFT is the most commonly known system of its type, the Clearing House Interbank Payment System (CHIPS) processes over $200 billion a day. In fact, "in three days, more dollars go through CHIPS than there are in the money supply of the US."[2]

---

[1] Jeffrey A. Frieden, "Banking on the World" p.103
[2] Ibid

This high volume is not only from international commerce; it is common practice for major US banks to place funds offshore overnight to capture higher rates. As exchange rates fluctuate instantaneously, the major processing systems work to seamlessly transfer funds throughout many nations and currencies.

Beyond considerations of currency exchange, an evaluation of an offshore jurisdiction should include a consideration of tax treaties or double-taxation agreements. These agreements provide taxpayers residing or conducting business abroad a foreign tax credit or deduction. According to the IRS, tax treaties accomplish a three part agenda: **"1) preventing the double taxation of income; 2) preventing discriminatory tax treatment of a resident of a treaty country; 3) permitting reciprocal administration to prevent tax avoidance and evasion."**[3] It is the responsibility of the Executive branch to establish tax treaties, while the Treasury "produces a technical explanation of a particular treaty. The Internal Revenue Service leans heavily upon this technical definition;" the definition varies in each individual case. Beyond basic tax negotiations, treaties may involve an exchange of information requirement between two countries. Here, the "coordination of administration serves to help prevent tax evasion."[4]

While U.S. tax treaties dictate interaction with American citizens, international information sharing initiatives have arisen to govern the global movement of money. Compliance with these organizations brings credibility and prestige to any offshore jurisdiction. One key regulating body is The Financial Action Task Force (FATF), commissioned by the G7. According to its charter, the G7 is charged with the, "development and promotion of

---

[3] IRS Rev. Proc. 91-23, 2.01, 1991-11 IRB 18.
[4] Joel D. Kuntz & Robert J. Peroni, "US International Taxation" vol. 2, C4.01[2]

policies, both at national and international levels, to combat money laundering and terrorist financing."[5] The FATF, based in Paris, does not directly regulate the banking systems of independent nations. Rather, the organization attempts to create the "necessary political will"[6] to bring about reform. The FATF has worked to legitimize IFC's by eliminating criminal activity to provide for healthy financial centers.

Similar to the FATF, the Organisation for Economic Co-operation and Development (OECD) is an international body formed of independent members. The OECD primarily serves to analyze the economies of many nations and recommend changes to increase prosperity, including recommendations for social and environmental change. Occasionally, negotiations "can culminate in formal agreements by countries, for example on combating bribery, on arrangements for export credits, or on the treatment of capital movements."[7] Of the more than 30 countries who are members of the OECD, most are first-world nations with large GDP's; however, smaller nations are welcomed through strategic partnerships with The Centre for Co-operation with Non-Members.

Currency exchange, tax treaties, and compliance with international governing bodies should be among the primary concerns when looking to an overseas financial center. What follows is a current, abbreviated profile on top financial centers meeting a vast array of personal criteria and preferences.

---

[5] www.fatf-gafi.org
[6] www.fatf-gafi.org
[7] www.oecd.org

Caribbean

Anguilla

Location:	Eastern Caribbean Sea
Capital City:	The Valley
Population:	13,500 (2008)
Language Spoken:	English
International Time:	EST + 1 hour
Airline Service:	American, US Airways, Continental, Delta, United
Currency:	Eastern Caribbean Dollar EC$2.70 = US$1
Type of Government:	Self-governing territory of the UK
Main industries:	Tourism, offshore incorporation and management, offshore banking, fishing
Tax Treaty:	No
OECD:	Approved
FATF:	Member CFATF [8]
Additional Notes:	Anguillan officials have put substantial effort into developing the offshore financial sector, which is small but growing.

Antigua and Barbuda

Location:	Eastern Caribbean Sea, 250 miles SE of Puerto Rico
Capital City:	St. Johns
Population:	82,000 (2008)
Language Spoken:	English
International Time:	EST + 1 hour
Airline Service:	Continental, Delta, American, US Airways, Windward Islands AIR
Currency:	Eastern Caribbean Dollar EC$2.70 = US$1

---

[8] The Caribbean Financial Action Task Force; partner of the FATF

Type of Government: Independent Parliamentary
                         Representative Democracy
Main industries: Tourism, manufacturing and
                         international banking
Tax Treaty: No
OECD: Approved
FATF: Member CFATF
Additional Notes: Have welcomed offshore banking
                         since 1982

Aruba

Location: Southern Caribbean Sea, 19 miles
                         from Venezuela mainland.
Capital City: Oranjstad
Population: 102,695 (2008)
Language Spoken: Dutch, Papiamento, English and
                         Spanish are also spoken.
International Time: EST + 1 hour
Airline Service: US Airways, United, Continental,
                         American, Air France
Currency: Arubin florin Af 1.8 = US$1
Type of Government: Member of the Commonwealth of
                         Nations; Independent Parliamentary
                         Democracy
Main industries: Tourism, oil refinery and storage,
                         offshore banking
Tax Treaty: Yes
OECD: Member
FATF: Member
Additional Notes: New legislation expected to be
                         approved in 2009; anticipated to
                         remain friendly to offshore formation

Bahamas

Location:	Caribbean, SE of Florida
Capital City:	Nassau
Population:	303,770 (2008)
Language Spoken:	English
International Time:	EST
Airline Service:	Air Canada, American, Bahamas Air, Continental, Northwest
Currency:	Bahamian Dollar B$1 = US$1
Type of Government:	member of the Commonwealth of Nations; Independent Parliamentary Democracy
Main industries:	Tourism and offshore banking and financial services
Tax Treaty:	No
OECD:	Approved
FATF:	Member CFATF
Additional Notes:	Highly favorable to offshore formation; even after new regulations, offshore business remains 15% of the GDP

Barbados

Location:	Eastern Caribbean
Capital City:	Bridgetown
Population:	281,968 (2008)
Language Spoken:	English
International Time:	EST + 1 hour
Airline Service:	Delta, US Airways, American, Caribbean Air, Air Canada
Currency:	Barbados BDS$2 = US$1
Type of Government:	Independent Constitutional Monarchy and Parliamentary Democracy

Main industries:	Agriculture, animal husbandry, fishing and mining
Tax Treaty:	No
OECD:	Approved
FATF:	Member CFATF
Additional Notes:	Offshore finance thrives due to time zone and educated workforce

Belize

Location:	Caribbean
Capital City:	Belmopan
Population:	301,270 (2008)
Language Spoken:	English, Creole, Spanish, Garifuna and Mayan are also spoken.
International Time:	EST + 2 hours
Airline Service:	American, Continental, US Airways, Delta
Currency:	Belizean dollar $2 = US$1
Type of Government:	Parliamentary democracy within the British Commonwealth; Member of the Commonwealth of Nations
Main industries:	Garment production, food processing, tourism and construction
Tax Treaty:	No
OECD:	Approved
FATF:	Member CFATF
Additional Notes:	Since 1995, offshore banks have been welcomed and regulated

Bermuda

Location:	Caribbean
Capital City:	Hamilton
Population:	65,365 (2008)
Language Spoken:	English

International Time: EST + 1 hour
Airline Service: Jet Blue, Air Canada, American, British Airways, Delta
Currency: Bermudian dollar Bd$ = US$1
Type of Government: British overseas territory with a high degree of internal self-government
Main industries: Offshore financial services, tourism, organized labor
Tax Treaty: Yes
OECD: Approved
FATF: Member CFATF
Additional Notes: Over 10% of the GCP is attributed to offshore financial activity, and many large corporations are headquartered here

British Virgin Islands

Location: Caribbean Sea (constitutes 36 islands)
Capital City: Road Town (Tortola)
Population: 21,730 (2008)
Language Spoken: English
International Time: Summer EST, Winter EST + 1 hour
Airline Service: American, US Airways, Continental
Currency: US$1 =US$1
Type of Government: British overseas territory with a high degree of internal self-government
Main industries: Tourism, offshore banking, livestock
Tax Treaty: Yes
OECD: Approved
FATF: Member CFATF
Additional Notes: Incorporation fees generate substantial revenue for the government; the adoption of comprehensive insurance law makes it an attractive option for Captives

Cayman Islands

Location:	460 miles South of Miami, Florida.
Capital City:	George Town
Population:	50,00 (2080)
Language Spoken:	English
International Time:	EST
Airline Service:	American, Cayman Airways, Delta, Northwest, Continental
Currency:	Cayman Islands dollar CI$
Type of Government:	British Crown Colony
Main industries:	Offshore financial services, tourism
Tax Treaty:	Yes
OECD:	Approved
FATF:	Member CFATF
Additional Notes:	The world's fifth largest financial service center after Hong Kong, London, New York and Tokyo. Currently over 500 Banks and 800 insurance companies reside here.

Costa Rica

Location:	Caribbean
Capital City:	San Jose
Population:	4.2M (2008)
Language Spoken:	Spanish
International Time:	CST
Airline Service:	LASCA (national airline), Air Canada, American, Avianca, Continental
Currency:	Colon
Type of Government:	Independent democratic republic
Main industries:	Tourism, agriculture and electronics exports
Tax Treaty:	Yes
OECD:	Approved

| FATF: | Member CFATF |
| Additional Notes: | Boasts political stability and high education levels as well as the fiscal incentives offered in free-trade zones |

Grenada

Location:	North of Trinidad and Tobago
Capital City:	St. George's
Population:	89,971 (2008)
Language Spoken:	English
International Time:	EST + 1 hour
Airline Service:	BWIA, Air France, Air Jamaica, American, Condor
Currency:	Eastern Caribbean dollar EC$2.70 =US$1
Type of Government:	Parliamentary Democracy
Main industries:	Tourism, construction, manufacturing, offshore incorporation
Tax Treaty:	Yes
OECD:	Approved
FATF:	Member CFATF
Additional Notes:	Government has intentionally planned for and welcomed an offshore financial sector

Netherland Antilles

Location:	30 miles off the NW coast of Venezuela
Capital City:	Willemstad
Population:	225,369 (2008)
Language Spoken:	Dutch, Papiamento, English and Spanish
International Time:	EST + 1 hour
Airline Service:	Air Canada, Air France, Air Jamaica,

	American, Jet Blue
Currency:	Netherlands Antilles florin Nafl 1.79 = US$1
Type of Government:	Autonomous country within the Kingdom of the Netherlands
Main industries:	Tourism, petroleum refining, offshore finance
Tax Treaty:	Yes
OECD:	Member
FATF:	Member
Additional Notes:	Enjoys a high per capita income and a well-developed infrastructure that welcomes offshore formation

Panama

Location:	Between Costa Rica and Colombia
Capital City:	Panama City
Population:	3,309,679 (2008)
Language Spoken:	English and Spanish
International Time:	EST
Airline Service:	Air Panama, Aero Mexico, American, Avianca, Mexicana
Currency:	Balboa
Type of Government:	Independent Constitutional Democracy
Main industries:	Operating the Panama Canal, banking, the Colon Free Zone, insurance, container ports, flagship registry, tourism
Tax Treaty:	No
OECD:	Approved
FATF:	Member CFATF
Additional Notes:	Panamanian Corporations are created under the General Corporation Law (32).

Law 32 has been used as a model for other offshore jurisdictions as it offers flexibility, structure, privacy, and legitimacy.

St. Vincent and the Grenadines

Location:	Caribbean Sea
Capital City:	Kingstown
Population:	118,432 (2008)
Language Spoken:	English
International Time:	EST + 1 hour
Airline Service:	LIAT, American, Delta, Air France, Air Berlin, British Airways
Currency:	Eastern Caribbean dollar EC$2.70 = US$1
Type of Government:	Parliamentary Democracy
Main industries:	Agriculture, tourism, construction
Tax Treaty:	Yes
OECD:	Approved
FATF:	Member CFATF
Additional Notes:	Home to a small offshore banking sector and has moved to adopt international regulatory standards

Turks and Caicos

Location:	575 miles SE of Miami
Capital City:	Grand Turk
Population:	22,352 (2008)
Language Spoken:	English
International Time:	EST
Airline Service:	Atlantic Gulf Airlines, American, British Airways, Delta, Frontier
Currency:	US dollar
Type of Government:	British Crown Colony

Main industries:	Tourism, offshore financial services, fishing
Tax Treaty:	Yes
OECD:	Approved
FATF:	Member
Additional Notes:	Offshore financial activities serve as a major source of government revenue

South Pacific

Cook Islands

Location:	1850 miles NE of New Zealand
Capital City:	Avarua
Population:	12,271 (2008)
Language Spoken:	English
International Time:	EST + 16 1/2 hours
Airline Service:	Air New Zealand, Cook Islands International, United, US Airways, Air France
Currency:	New Zealand dollar
Type of Government:	Self-governing territory of the United Kingdom
Main industries:	Agriculture and manufacturing
Tax Treaty:	Yes
OECD:	Approved
FATF:	Approved
Additional Notes:	Passed legislation in the early 1980s that allows for a high degree of flexibility, simplicity and administrative ease for offshore sector

Hong Kong

Location:	90 miles S of Canton
Capital City:	ictoria
Population:	7.1M (2008)

Language Spoken:	Chinese (Cantonese), English
International Time:	EST + 13 hours
Airline Service:	Air Canada, Air China, American, Delta, and 30+ other international airlines
Currency:	Hong Kong dollar
Type of Government:	Special administrative region of China with a limited democracy
Main industries:	Highly dependent on international trade and financial sector
Tax Treaty:	No
OECD:	Approved
FATF:	Member
Additional Notes:	One of the world's largest international banking centers with a well-regulated offshore sector

Singapore

Location:	On the Straits of Malacca
Capital City:	Singapore
Population:	4.8M (2008)
Language Spoken:	Chinese, Malay, Tamil, English all official
International Time:	EST + 13 hours
Airline Service:	United Airlines, Singapore Airlines, American, US Airways, Asiana, Delta
Currency:	Singapore dollar
Type of Government:	Independent Parliamentary Republic
Main industries:	International trade economy focusing on consumer electronics and information technology products
Tax Treaty:	Yes
OECD:	Approved
FATF:	Member

Additional Notes:	One of the lowest tax rates in Asia and expects to see large growth in offshore banking due to favorable tax treaties with the EU

Vanuatu

Location:	500 miles W of Fiji
Capital City:	Port Vila
Population:	215, 446 (2008)
Language Spoken:	Bislama, English and French
International Time:	EST + 16 hours
Airline Service:	Air Vanuatu, Air New Guinea, American, Delta, Continental, Air Pacific
Currency:	Vatu
Type of Government:	Independent Parliamentary Republic
Main industries:	Small-scale agriculture, fishing, shipping registration
Tax Treaty:	No
OECD:	Approved
FATF:	Approved
Additional Notes:	Recently passed new regulation of the offshore sector that allows for greater international acceptance

Europe

Gibraltar

Location:	Southern most part of Spain
Capital City:	Gibraltar
Population:	28,002 (2008)
Language Spoken:	French, Spanish, English
International Time:	EST + 6 hours
Airline Service:	British Airways, Gibraltar Airways
Currency:	Gibraltar pound

Type of Government:	British Crown Colony, parliamentary democracy
Main industries:	Depends on shipping trade and tourism for international conferences
Tax Treaty:	No
OECD:	Approved
FATF:	Member
Additional Notes:	The Gibraltar Compliance Ordinance has been enhanced to allow for many different types of offshore corporations

Guernsey

Location:	40 miles N of France
Capital City:	St. Peter Port
Population:	65,726 (2008)
Language Spoken:	English
International Time:	EST + 5 hours
Airline Service:	British Airways, Guernsey Air, Aurigny, Blue Island, Flybe, Skynet
Currency:	Pound
Type of Government:	British Crown Colony, parliamentary democracy
Main industries:	Financial services – banking, fund management, insurance – construction, retail, tourism, manufacturing, horticulture
Tax Treaty:	No
OECD:	Approved
FATF:	Member
Additional Notes:	Light tax and death duties make it a top tax haven

Ireland

Location:	West of Great Britain
Capital City:	Dublin

Population:	4.1M (2008)
Language Spoken:	English, Irish Gaelic
International Time:	EST + 5 hours
Airline Service:	Delta, Charter flights, Air Canada, Continental, British Airways
Currency:	Punt (pound)
Type of Government:	Parliamentary Republic
Main industries:	Agriculture and construction.
Tax Treaty:	Yes
OECD:	Member
FATF:	Approved
Additional Notes:	Many different financially-oriented companies obtain tax and fiscal advantages by locating themselves in Ireland

Isle of Man

Location:	In Irish Sea, 20 miles from Scotland
Capital City:	Douglas
Population:	76,220 (2008)
Language Spoken:	English
International Time:	EST + 5 hours
Airline Service:	Manx Airlines, British Airways
Currency:	Pound
Type of Government:	British Crown Colony, parliamentary democracy
Main industries:	Offshore banking, manufacturing, high-technology companies, tourism
Tax Treaty:	No
OECD:	Approved
FATF:	Member
Additional Notes:	Government provides incentive to technology companies and financial institutions to locate on the island

Jersey

Location:	Off the coast of France
Capital City:	St. Helier
Population:	91,533 (2008)
Language Spoken:	English
International Time:	EST + 5 hours
Airline Service:	British Airways, BMI, US Airways
Currency:	British Pound
Type of Government:	British Crown Colony, parliamentary democracy
Main industries:	International financial services, agriculture and tourism
Tax Treaty:	No
OECD:	Approved
FATF:	Member
Additional Notes:	Light taxes and death duties make the island a popular tax haven

Liechtenstein

Location:	Central Europe
Capital City:	Vaduz
Population:	34,498 (2008)
Language Spoken:	German
International Time:	EST + 6 hours
Airline Service:	American, Air service from Austria or Switzerland
Currency:	Swiss franc
Type of Government:	Independent Constitutional Monarchy; participates in a customs union with Switzerland and uses the Swiss franc as its national currency
Main industries:	Financial service center with large number of small, diverse companies
Tax Treaty:	No

OECD:	On the OECD List of Uncooperative Tax Havens
FATF:	Has undertaken steps to implement regulation, but is still not approved
Additional Notes:	Relationship with Switzerland, los business taxes, and easy incorporation rules make this a favorable offshore jurisdiction

Luxembourg

Location:	Western Europe
Capital City:	Luxembourg City
Population:	486,006
Language Spoken:	German, French, Luxembourgish, English
International Time:	EST + 6 hours
Airline Service:	Luxair, Air France, British Airways, Lufthansa, Continental, Delta
Currency:	Lux franc
Type of Government:	Constitutional Monarchy
Main industries:	Industry, finance and agriculture
Tax Treaty:	Yes
OECD:	Member
FATF:	Member
Additional Notes:	Financial services sector accounts for 28% of the GDP

Malta

Location:	Mediterranean
Capital City:	Valetta
Population:	401,880 (2008)
Language Spoken:	Maltese, English
International Time:	EST + 6 hours
Airline Service:	Air Europe, Air Malta, British Islands

	Airways, Monarch Airlines
Currency:	Lira
Type of Government:	Independent Republic
Main industries:	Dependent on foreign trade, manufacturing of electronics and pharmaceuticals and tourism
Tax Treaty:	Yes
OECD:	Approved
FATF:	Approved
Additional Notes:	Advanced legislation has introduced two distinct offshore structure which take advantage of tax treaties

Monaco

Location:	Heart of French Riviera
Capital City:	Monaco-Villa
Population:	32,796
Language Spoken:	English, French, Italian, Monegasque
International Time:	EST + 6 hours
Airline Service:	Serviced by airport in Nice, France; American, British Airways, Air Canada
Currency:	French franc
Type of Government:	Independent Hereditary and Constitutional Monarchy
Main industries:	Resort and tourism, offshore banking and finance
Tax Treaty:	No
OECD:	On the OECD List of Uncooperative Tax Havens
FATF:	Approved
Additional Notes:	No income tax and low business taxes make this a tax haven for individuals who have established residence or foreign companies here

Switzerland

Location:	Central Europe (landlocked)
Capital City:	Bern
Population:	7.7M (2008)
Language Spoken:	French, Italian, German, Romansch
International Time:	EST + 6 hours
Airline Service:	Swissair, British Airways, American, Air Canada, Continental
Currency:	Franc
Type of Government:	Federal Republic
Main industries:	Flourishing financial services sector
Tax Treaty:	Yes
OECD:	Member
FATF:	Member
Additional Notes:	Has conformed regulations to enhance prestige but remains a safe haven for investor because it maintains unparalleled bank secrecy

Conclusion

This list represents only a sampling of the many offshore markets that exist in today's global economy. Certainly, there have been scandals offshore just as there have been in domestic financial markets. Despite a relative few incidents, mostly before the age of increased regulations, the countries in this chapter represent a yearly cumulative Gross National Product of greater than $400 billion. The narrow-minded view held by many people, especially in America, that offshore financial business is somehow illegal or unfavorable ignores the simple fact that "offshore financial markets ... are a major force in the economies of all the world's nations. No corporation, investor or government is insulated from trends in international banking."[1] Doing business overseas means taking advantage of the same benefits that many major corporations use daily. As individuals and companies reject the concept that the boundaries of their nation should be the boundaries of their business, offshore financial centers will only increase in number, significance and potential benefits.

---

[1] Jeffrey A. Frieden, "Banking on the World" p.103

Chapter 7

"Types of Offshore Vehicles"

The term "offshore vehicle" does not describe one single type of entity. Rather, there are six major types of offshore vehicles, each with very different benefits. Successfully acquiring or establishing an offshore vehicle requires an understanding of the benefits the business or individual is looking to obtain. For example, US citizens hoping to obtain tax relief via offshore vehicles will encounter many hurdles purposely put in place to stop such a move. Citizens of other countries, however, are likely to find that benefit much easier to obtain. Rarely is tax relief the main motivation in obtaining an international financial institution. Understanding the differing benefits of each unique offshore vehicle will lead to more success in obtaining the anticipated benefits.

International Business Corporations

A time-tested form of offshore vehicle, International Business Corporations, also known as IBC's, are corporations established under the legislation of an offshore jurisdiction. Often considered a versatile and inexpensive alternative to Delaware Corporations in the United States, they are similar in requiring only a small presence actually maintained in the host country. Just as with most Delaware Corporations, a representative office established and maintained by a local law firm is usually sufficient. Despite minimal local presence, IBC's offer a wide-range of benefits.

"We are not afraid to entrust the American people with unpleasant facts, foreign ideas, alien philosophies and competitive values. For a nation that is afraid to let its people judge the truth and falsehood in an open market is afraid of its people."
- John F. Kennedy (1962)

A key feature with any offshore vehicle is privacy. Few regulatory requirements for IBC's mean, in most cases, the only aspects of an IBC that are or can become a matter of public record are the incorporation documents listing the registered office and agent. Thus, the owners of the IBC are not widely known, and, ultimately, privacy is maintained. A few countries still allow for bearer shares, an equity security that is owned by whoever is in possession of the physical certificate. Bearer shares are not subject to the guidelines of common shares because ownership is never recorded. In the United States, tax free municipal bonds were traded in bearer shares. Some may remember cutting off the coupons attached to tax free bonds to collect interest. The ownership of these bonds was not registered; therefore, they were frequently kept in safety deposit boxes since possession was like cash. In the 1980s, when the U.S. Government sought knowledge of who owned their debt, this option was eliminated. The benefits of bearer shares, where applicable, offer an additional layer of privacy.

Using an IBC can result in many advantages in addition to privacy. **Again, please keep in mind that taxes and reporting requirements will vary depending upon the jurisdictions involved and the types of transactions. You should thoroughly understand your country's obligations before structuring offshore.** Uses and benefits may include:

■   **Trading:** The trading of various goods is often routed through an offshore jurisdiction to minimize tax. This can be a controversial strategy and is frequently referred to as "invoicing through" a specific country.

■ **Portfolio Management:** Stocks, bonds, mutual funds precious metals and commodities can be traded through an offshore IBC. Performance may be enhanced since more opportunities exist internationally and your domestic regulatory body may prohibit their entry.

■ **Equipment Leasing:** Title to machinery and equipment can be held offshore by an IBC. Additionally, profits from the operation can be maintained offshore as well.

■ **Ship Registration:** Ships are frequently registered abroad to minimize tax and liability. In addition, costs can be lowered when utilizing personnel from developing countries.

■ An IBC **may not** act as a Trust, Bank or Insurance Company. It is often restricted from doing business with the local citizens, thus, it may also be referred to as an exempt company. Many countries will also restrict it from owning local real estate.

Many corporations are currently enjoying the advantages of IBC's. For example, in the Cayman Islands there are approximately 30,000 companies registered. Bermuda has over 9,000 registered international companies; British Virgin Islands has 200,000 and the Bahamas lists another 65,000.

Today, one of the most utilized jurisdictions for the establishment of IBC's remains the Bahamas. Lying sixty miles off the southeast coast of Florida, the Bahamas is a collection of 700 islands and cays, stretching more than 500 miles in length. Numerous factors have contributed to this small country's important position; primary among those considerations is its stability. An independent nation within the British Commonwealth of Nations, the Bahamas has enjoyed an uninterrupted 260-year reign of political democracy, peace and prosperity. Only a 30-minute flight from the United States, there are no income taxes, no corporate income taxes, no death duties or inheritance taxes, no sales tax and no capital gains tax. The cost to establish a Bahamian IBC is likely to run in the range of $1,000 to $1,200 for bare bones incorporation. This tax-free environment, total commitment to confidentiality, and centuries-old political and economic stability make the Bahamas one of the best offshore jurisdictions.

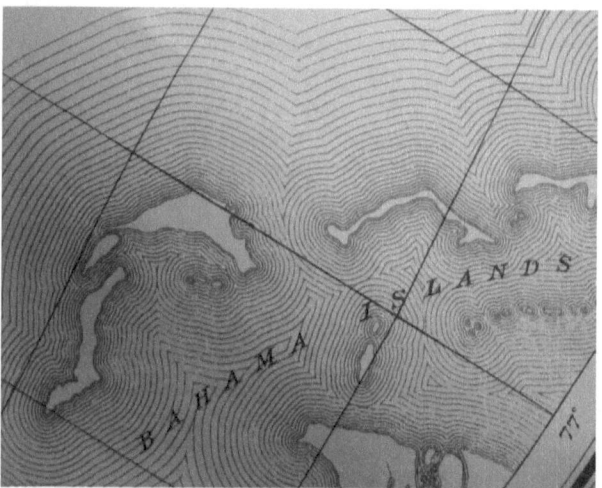

With the many nuances in jurisdiction and anticipated benefits, anyone considering the establishment of an IBC should consider using a consulting service. Cost savings are usually possible because of volume discounts afforded to these firms. In most cases, if contacted during normal working hours, a corporate name reservation can be accomplished within a mere 15 minutes.

Asset Protection Trusts

Asset Protection Trusts, or APT's, are complex structures that can be custom made to fit the needs of a particular individual and his or her goals. The history of wealthy families using trusts dates back to Roman times when trusts were used as an instrument for holding property. More recently, trusts were common in England as early as the 11th century. It is generally accepted that the modern trust, used for asset protection and estate planning, has a history extending some four hundred years.

In the United States, it was possible to obtain substantial tax benefits prior to the Tax Reform Act of 1976. "Under prior law, a United States citizen could create an irrevocable accumulation trust that would be taxed in basically the same manner as a nonresident alien individual. Thus, it was possible to defer United States taxes indefinitely or until distributions were actually made to its US beneficiaries."[1] While tax law reform has eroded much of the tax-planning power of the trust in United States, it remains a powerful tax planning weapon elsewhere. For citizens of the United States, the Offshore Asset Protection Trust is a formidable tool for asset protection against creditors and litigators.

An APT with the objective of protecting assets should divest the settler of just sufficient ownership of assets to deter potential future claims by creditors or litigators. For United States' citizens, ownership of a foreign trust will frustrate the efforts of creditors as assets are the property of a trust and not a named individual. Offshore courts are hesitant to set aside a transfer to a trust if it is properly established under their law. In addition, a judgment from a U.S. litigator is difficult to enforce offshore; most litigation stops at the border. If for any reason the jurisdiction was

---

[1] Marshall J. Langer, "Practical International Tax Planning" p.57

approached and asked to disallow the trust, it can easily be moved to another country before any such an action would take effect.

Much like any offshore consideration, anyone considering an offshore trust should seek the advice of a competent, professional advisor. There are several terms regarding trusts that your advisor will use frequently:

- **Settlor** or **Grantor**: A person placing property into a trust.
- **Trustee**: The professional who manages the trust for those named as beneficiaries.
- **Beneficiary**: Individual(s) named to benefit from the trust.

Finally, it is important to keep in mind that there are many types of trusts. One specific type of trust cannot be all things to all people. The best approach is to know your main objective, and then consult a professional.

Offshore Mutual Funds

Most offshore mutual fund managers are interested in two distinct benefits: privacy and reduced regulatory filings and oversight.

In order to be competitive within the global economy, certain nations have recognized that it is in their best interests to be as accommodating to the financial industry as possible. International financial centers that predominately offer attractive mutual funds or investment company regulations are concentrated in the Caribbean, Europe and the South Pacific. The task of disseminating all relevant foreign source information and weaving through a web of complicated and frequently subtle jurisdictional differences is arduous at best. The end result is some nations are more attractive for specific projects than are others.

Chartered under the laws of those countries considered pro-business, offshore funds are fully recognized by the international investment community. In addition, they offer significant advantages when compared to their domestic counterparts. Most funds can be fully established within a 4-6 week time frame and often with fewer regulatory restrictions. The range of potential portfolio investments is also much greater. The ability to transact business tax-free in the host country, with little red tape and in a private manner, offers a tremendous advantage.

According to various reports, in the U.S. market alone, almost $2 trillion dollars are invested in domestic mutual funds. Each day another $1 million dollars gets placed in this area of investment with at least 28% of all households having ownership. Over 8,000 domestic mutual funds are now in business, predominately comprised of portfolios with stocks, bonds or a mixture of both. Exact international numbers are difficult to obtain due to the privacy element. It is apparent, however, the international market is similar to the US in that the most popular objective remains managing these specialized mixed portfolios. Many international fund managers are traders, brokers or analysts, confident that their methods can produce superior returns for investors.

"One doesn't discover new lands without consenting to lose sight of the shore for a very long time."
-Andre Gide

The international market offers numerous opportunities; for example, exploring to discover natural resources such as oil and natural gas provides incentive. The ability to engage in two different geographic markets lends itself to securities or currency arbitrage activities. Real estate projects in the United States and elsewhere can raise funds internationally. Rental properties can also be obtained through a fund. Finally, projects that may have exotic objectives can also be accomplished offshore. This would include interests in professional tennis players, golfers, entertainers, race horses and even the recovery of sunken treasure. In recent years, even the financing of motion pictures has been taken offshore.

Please note that all marketing solicitations for offshore mutual funds must be outside of the U.S. and Canada. All other key factors for operation which would include administrative aspects, mail forwarding, fax communications, shareholder services and processing can be referred to an appropriate international management firm located offshore.

Any listing of who's who in offshore funds is extremely prestigious. A few examples follow:

John Templeton, best known as the founder of the Templeton group which includes numerous domestically based mutual funds. His first fund, the "Templeton Growth Fund" was founded in 1954. Mr. Templeton has long been one of the industry's most highly regarded figures. Since the 1960's, much of the Templeton operation has been maintained internationally in the Bahamas.

George Soros, founder of the "Quantum Fund" with estimated assets over $2 billion, is one of the world's largest funds and is domiciled offshore. Mr. Soros is also one of the most respected figures in the investment industry and one of the world's largest philanthropists.

Merrill Lynch, which was acquired by Bank of America in 2008, is one of the United States' best known brokerage firms, holding numerous offshore funds. American Express, Scudder, Meridian and Fidelity represent additional household names with ownership of various offshore funds. These are just a few of the well known American corporate names that have offshore interests. Virtually, every domestically based financial institution has substantial holdings internationally.

Licensing expenditures and requirements vary from jurisdiction to jurisdiction. Initial expenditures will run a minimum of $18,000 to establish the fund structure with annual fees of approximately $3,000. It is also required to designate whether the fund will be closely held or publicly traded; this will have an impact upon expenditures.

Offshore Hedge Funds

Similar to a domestic hedge fund, an offshore hedge fund is an aggressively managed portfolio of investments that uses advanced investment strategies such as leverage, long, short and derivative positions in an overseas jurisdiction with the goal of generating high returns (either in an absolute sense or over a specified market benchmark). The main advantages to this type of offshore vehicle are less regulatory oversight than domestic hedge funds and an increased ability to work with groups of international investors.

Offshore Insurance Companies

Also known as Captive Insurance Companies, offshore insurance companies have as an important part of the global insurance industry. Over the last twenty-five years, multinational corporations and professionals have looked to captives to provide protection against risk while lowering costs. In recent years, private citizens have also looked offshore for these same benefits.

A captive is defined as an insurance company established in an offshore jurisdiction, created and controlled by either a parent company or professional association through which their own risk is insured. Those insured risks are frequently reinsured through a large multinational carrier.

Recently, the subject of insurance has become a "hot" topic in the news. The reason? For industries such as special events, sports and commercial real estate, being able to obtain insurance has become elusive; especially when there is the threat of future terrorism.

Highly publicized events and athletics are in need of such coverage due to the exposure they receive. The Dow Jones reported on February 7, 2002, that neither the US Olympic committee nor Salt Lake City had been able to obtain adequate coverage to cover lawsuits in case athletes, organizers or visitors were injured. In that same month, the Dow Jones again ran a statement issued by a spokesperson for the Miami Dolphins who said the team does not have any terrorism insurance, and other NFL teams are encountering the same difficulties. Reuters wire service reported in January 2008 that, if the organizers for the Oscar awards ceremony in March could not get enough insurance, the event may not occur as planned.

Beyond elaborate sport and entertainment venues, real estate and commercial lending have been notably hard hit by the inability to obtain adequate coverage for existing commercial property, new construction and various other potential terrorist targets according to congressional studies. The House Financial Services Committee released a report on Tuesday February 26, 2002, stating, "…it is still unclear to what extent financing arrangements for existing or planned projects will be jeopardized as lenders and investors are faced with the prospect of absorbing additional terrorism-related risks that cannot be insured."

Purchases of major commercial properties are being obstructed by lenders since insurance companies are either not offering insurance against terrorist attacks or charging exorbitant premiums (some have increased premiums up to 400%) and then limiting the scope of policies, making the cost unreasonable. In previous editorials, both USA Today and the Wall Street Journal have addressed these difficulties. USA Today explored how some companies are insuring themselves against terrorism saying, "…the specter of future attacks, and the inability to predict their scope and frequency have caused insurers to back away from terrorism coverage." The Wall Street Journal further revisited the topic pertaining to commercial property and terrorism indicating that "…owners and buyers of some trophy properties are still finding coverage difficult to get or extremely expensive…" Companies and property owners could find themselves in default for loans and mortgages if they lose their terrorism coverage.

"Over 350 of the Fortune 500 companies have captive insurance companies in Bermuda."

Amidst all these obstacles, there are many options to consider. One is to discontinue insurance coverage if the premiums do not cover essentials, which could be disastrous. Another is to accept the terms of the insurance company with the heavy premiums and minimal coverage, which does not make good business sense. Lastly is the option to acquire an offshore captive insurance company and self-insure.

More than ever, the use of captive insurance companies is now being seen as an integral and affordable part of general business risk management. Typically, captives are acquired to insure the risks of the parent company and do not accept risks from outside parties. The types of captives are defined as follows:

- **Single Parent Captive:** Insurance Company which is a wholly owned subsidiary.
- **Association Captive:** Insurance Company owned by a trade industry or group for the benefit of its members.
- **Group Captive:** Insurance Company jointly owned by a number of companies created to meet a common need.
- **Rent-a-Captive:** Owner of a captive offers insurance services to those interested for a fee.

The driving force behind the move to offshore captives is the ever-upward spiral of insurance costs. This trend extends virtually across all industries including, but not limited to, medical malpractice, workers compensation, manufacturing, financial, energy-related, and real estate developers, just to name a few. Over 350 of the Fortune 500 companies in the United States have insurance captives located in Bermuda. Many others have captives located elsewhere.

Costs to establish a captive vary considerably. Licensing costs range from $18,000 to $100,000. Paid-in-capital requirements, which are funds posted for the benefit of the offshore entity will also be encountered. Paid-in-capital will likely range from $250,000 to well into seven figures. The bottom line is that captive insurance companies can be a very valuable tool but certainly are not inexpensive to establish and operate.

While the benefits of owning a captive are vast, in some cases, it may be the first step for the parent company to enter into the insurance business. Therefore, quality planning is critical to maximize advantages and properly shift risk to the captive. In addition, many tax advantages exist, but, can be very difficult to obtain in the United States. A good tax advisor familiar with the captive insurance industry is a necessity.

Offshore Private Banks

Broadly defined, Private International Banks (PIB's), Offshore Banks or Captive Banks are simply banking entities established outside of the United States or the country in which the owner resides. In most cases, these entities are not subject to state, federal or other domestic regulations. The advantage of avoiding costly regulations, such as reserve and insurance requirements, can result in a path of profits contributing directly to the bottom line. There are two distinct types of international banks:

- **Class A Banks**

    A Class A bank is typically a storefront business operation, often accompanied by a marquee. It is a combination banking entity, accepting public deposits for both private and business accounts. In the United Sates, we are most familiar with the Class A bank. This type of banking license is held by all the "majors" and frequently has the customary vault, tellers and ATM machines. Examples of international Class A banks would include Credite Suisse, Barclays & Royal Bank of Canada.

- **Class B Banks**

    The second type of international bank is a "Class B" bank or a "Private International Bank." This bank is usually restricted from doing business with the citizens of the host country and does not maintain a presence on "the street". A representative, usually an attorney, will post a brass plate on their office building exterior and all business is conducted via fax, telephone and mail. Class B banks are

are able to issue virtually all of the same financial instruments as that of a Class A bank; however, they should not provide services to citizens of the host country. All solicitations need to be carefully monitored. Advertisements are restricted to the appropriate international periodicals. Private International Banks tend to have higher profit margins and lower capital outlays.

Private International Banks also allow for international financial matters to be transacted in complete privacy, free from host country taxation, without exchange controls and without the need to ever leave your country of residence. Only a minimal presence need be established within the borders of the host nation.

- **Captive Banks**
    Ownership of a Captive Bank should be viewed as an entrepreneurial endeavor. A Private Bank is a dynamic tool, requiring a special license, in order to capitalize on overseas business environments. Captives have many possible functions including: securities trading, deposit taking and merchant banking. In addition to offering the

owner a commercial endeavor, secondary benefits of privacy and asset protection are also possible. Tax benefits are best pursued by non US citizens. The investment range to obtain one-hundred percent ownership of a captive bank is in the range of $35,000 to $10 million.

During the mid-1960's, the offshore market experienced tremendous growth due to several events. These events were highlighted by the introduction of new bank instruments and restrictive measures implemented by the U.S., making offshore dollar borrowing highly attractive. Perhaps most importantly, familiarity with the offshore market grew. The result was a dramatic increase in the total number of Class A and Class B banks worldwide. From this legacy, the global financial culture has inherited a significant offshore bank sector that continues to thrive.

Conclusion

There are six major types of offshore vehicles; benefits of ownership vary depending on the institution. These institutions are rarely the only component in a business plan. More likely, they are tools to enact a greater financial plan of a business or individual. Ultimately, success depends on the overall business plan and the strategic use of an offshore financial institution in its execution. When you are seeking specific advantages in an offshore vehicle, expert advice on the proper type of institution for the advantages sought is integral in acquiring with purpose and realizing your goals.

"Great spirits have always found violent opposition from mediocre minds. The latter cannot understand it when a man does not thoughtlessly submit to hereditary prejudices but honestly and courageously uses his intelligence."
- Albert Einstein

Chapter 8

"Banks Are Unique"

Principals of Bank Ownership

If you wish to transact any business on behalf of third parties, you will need a bank. What constitutes transacting business for a third party? The answer is any action taken on behalf of or with another that is financial in nature. A few examples of transacting business for a third party include providing loans, trading securities, writing debt obligations and issuing letters of credit. While some of these functions can be accomplished through non-banking entities, essentially, bank ownership offers more avenues for use than any other type of entity. Keep in mind the specific uses of the various vehicles. Corporations provide a veil of protection and privacy. Trusts are a good means of securing asset protection. Insurance companies are terrific at providing insurance services to a captive clientele. Private Banks can frequently include most of these functions and many more.

"The gratification of wealth is not found in mere possession or in lavish expenditure, but in its wise application."
– Miguel de Cervantes

Introduction to Bank Ownership

Private Bank Ownership can be obtained both domestically and internationally. Choosing whether to acquire a domestic or international bank involves selecting a location most favorable to your personal goals. While each independent jurisdiction has specific regulation and entry requirements, there are basic differences between domestic and international banks that will determine which option is right for you.

Domestic Bank Ownership *(Within the U.S.)*

U.S. banks offer owners the opportunity to directly work with and market to United States' citizens. While many international banks can accomplish this goal to a degree, they will meet regulatory boundaries in some cases. If you must market to the American general public, domestic ownership may be right for you. However, owning a domestic bank means meeting the rules and regulations of the United States—considered one of the most watchful and transparent banking systems in the world.

"Most investors say "don't take risks." The rich investor takes risks."

– Robert Kiyosaki

Chartering a bank within the United States typically follows the De Novo Bank Application process. The process in its entirety can cost an average of USD$5 million and take up to 36 months to complete. The De Novo Bank Application process is supervised by the Federal Reserve and consists of a highly public supervisory process including answering key questions related to the purpose and services associated with the new charter.

A few important items to consider before applying include:

1)   The type of charter desired (State or Federal)
2)   Whether the charter will serve independently or if a bank holding company will have ownership.
3)   Regulatory fees to charter, operate & maintain the entity.

Offshore Bank Ownership (Outside the U.S.)

If your business goals can be accomplished through an international structure, you can substantially reduce costs compared to a domestic acquisition. Again, broadly defined, "Private International Banks" (PIB's) or "Offshore Banks" are simply banking entities established outside of the United States or the country in which the depositor resides. Thus, in most cases these entities are not subject to State or Federal rules or regulations. The advantage of avoiding costly regulations such as reserve and insurance requirements results in a path of profits contributing directly to the bottom line.

The tremendous increase in popularity of private international banking over the past two decades is proof that the special benefits provided by such entities are not only acceptable but have become commonplace for major corporations, entrepreneurs and individual investors. Virtually every domestic-based financial institution maintains interests offshore, either through private banking or mutual fund securities. Beyond financial institutions, numerous companies typically associated with American business also enjoy the benefits of offshore ownership. Merrill Lynch, American Express, Firestone, Dow Chemical and Bank of America are just a few of the well-known names with substantial offshore interests.

Keep in mind that there are approximately fifty jurisdictions around the world which, in one form or another, can be classified as International Financial Centers (IFCs). Please refer back to Chapter Six for detailed information related to many of these well-known IFCs. The Banking Systems in these highlighted jurisdictions reflect the different cultures and ideals of their citizens. As a result, there are numerous variations to private banking, each location enforcing its own rules, regulations, benefits and customs. It is important to note that one jurisdiction will not work for all. Outlining your specific goals and qualifications is a necessary step prior to deciding the best strategy to implement. To suggest otherwise is to do you a disservice.

"Diversification is protection against ignorance."
– Warren Buffet

Basic Classifications of Offshore Banks

While the oversight body of each specific jurisdiction determines the types of offshore financial institutions it will welcome, there are a few general types of international banks. When first regulated, the general types of international banks were Class A, Class B and Class C. "Class A" banks were recognizable as a storefront business operation often accompanied by a marquee where retail traffic could enter and do business. "Class B" banks or "Private International Banks" were open to international business, but were restricted from doing business with the citizens of the host country, and no presence was maintained on "the street". "Class C" banks, or "restricted" banks, were restricted to doing business only with named shareholders of the bank. These classifications have been restructured in recent years.

Today, Class I and Class II banking licenses are widely available. Within Class I, banks fall into two general categories: Unrestricted and Restricted. "Class I Unrestricted" banks echo the structures of the former Class A category; these are retail banks open for business with the general public including citizens of the host country. "Class I Restricted" banks are similar to former Class B banks. They are open to international clientele and networks but do not take business from citizens of the host country. A Class II banking license is a restricted license similar to the former Class C license. Banks which fall under this category are restricted to doing business only with named and approved shareholders. Class II banks generally serve as internal financial networks for a company's subsidiaries.

As each class of bank is set up to assist a distinct demographic of clientele, it is essential to know these restrictions and choose appropriately before beginning any acquisition or application process.

The Six Components of PIB's

Each type of bank, Class A or Class B, has six major components that contribute to making the entity operational. The basic components are:

1) **Bank Charter and License:** Legal framework for the bank. Establishes the bank's authority and distinguishes the difference between a financial institution and a corporation.
2) **Registered Office:** Representative office in the host country.
3) **Resident Agent:** Local liaison.

4) **Board of Directors:** Usually from one to ten people that hold meetings and direct bank business.

5) **Shareholders:** PIB owners.

6) **Clearing Accounts:** An account with a major bank or brokerage.

Direct Benefits

The exact benefits a bank provides its owner relies heavily on the use of the private bank in a focused business plan. In any case, regardless of business plan, every offshore bank offers a few major benefits. In general, the basic benefits afforded to the owner of a private offshore bank include:

- **Privacy** - Strict bank privacy laws shield records of financial institutions from unwarranted probes. By owning a Private International Bank (PIB) under favorable privacy laws, you are virtually insured against financial intrusions that have become all too common.
- **Profit** - All banking institutions, foreign and domestic, borrow funds from their depositors at a low rate and lend it out to their borrowers at a higher rate. Therefore, PIB owners profit from opportunities of money manipulation available only to banks.
- **Asset Protection** - Dependent upon the structure, assets placed in the banking entity may be immune to judgments, seizures and other judicial writs.
- **Diversification of Personal Assets** - Your personal portfolio can be held offshore and maintained in accounts with familiar

correspondent banks located in major international financial centers, opening up a world of potential investment vehicles not available in the United States. Historically, U.S. markets have provided mediocre returns compared to international alternatives.

Potential Business Strategies

To enjoy benefits beyond the basic four mentioned above, you should carefully consider your business plan. A targeted business plan for a private bank may be an extension of your ongoing business or a new consideration. Some of the most successful strategies include:

- Offering Secured Credit Cards
- Credit, Debit, Prepaid Cards and ACH Transfers
- Cost Reduction for Credit & Debit Card Processing
- Providing Confidential Accounts
- Offering Private Client Services
- Selling Offshore Securities
- Structuring Venture Capital
- Holding and Expanding Real Estate
- Research and Development Activities
- Assisting in Foreign Trade
- Registering Aircraft
- Manufacturing
- Shipping

"If you want to make money, go where the money is."
– Joseph P. Kennedy

Bank Authority

Employing and developing your business plan legally requires an understanding of the authorities you are afforded as an offshore bank. Offshore banks are typically able to participate in the following major activities. Restrictions vary and the listing provided below is not all inclusive:

- Deposit Taking and Lending
- Offering Securities
- Cash management Services
- Payment Services
- Term Deposits
- Wire transfer Services
- Broker Mortgages
- Investment Banking Functions
- Acquire & Hold Real Estate
- Borrow From Third Parties
- Loan To Third Parties
- Portfolio Management
- Private Bank Services
- Wholesale Bank Services
- Buy & Sell Precious Metals For Third Parties
- Buy & Sell Precious Stones For Third Parties
- Issue Credit & Debit Cards
- Issue Equity Securities
- Issue Bonds
- Issue Debentures
- Issue Bank Guarantees
- Issue Letters of Credit
- Issue Numbered Accounts
- Deal in Goodwill
- Insurance Brokerage
- Broker Offshore Annuities
- Act as a Trustee
- Provide Confidential Accounts
- Deal in Shipping
- Deal in Precious Metal Markets
- Commodities Brokerage
- Establish Corresponding Banking Relationships
- Hold Patents
- Arbitrage Activities
- Euro Dollar Activities

"If we command our wealth, we shall be rich and free; if our wealth commands us, we are poor indeed."
– Unknown

Conclusion

Private bank ownership does not mean one thing to all people. With the various considerations of domestic versus international, Class A versus Class B and the nuances of regulation and establishment as they apply to jurisdiction, the private bank map can be difficult to navigate. When structuring your private bank, it is important to begin with the basics; deciding on your preferred business plan and strategies should always be your first step. Once you have determined your ideal situation, seek the advice of an expert to assist you in deciding which options will bring about the results and solutions you are seeking.

Chapter 9

*"Private Trust Companies, an Alternative to
Bank Ownership"*

Introduction
In addition to private international banks, as outlined in the
previous chapter, many jurisdictions have legislation
allowing for the formation or acquisition of private trust
companies (PTCs). A trust company, by definition, is a
registered entity that acts as fiduciary, agent or trustee for a
person or business unit for the reason of administration,
management and the ultimate relocation of assets to a
beneficial party.

A Private Trust Company differs from an Asset Protection Trust
The general public, typically, relates the term "trust" with
Asset Protection Trusts, Foreign Situs Trusts, Irrevocable
Trusts or perhaps Real Estate Investment Trusts. PTCs,
however, are an entirely different type of institution. Far
beyond asset protection trusts, private trust companies
can and do serve as business expansion tools offering
financial services to their beneficial owners and clients. In
this capacity, private trust companies are organized for
the purpose of performing broad and discretionary
fiduciary, administrative and financial services to their
shareholders, related subsidiaries and clients. The scope
of services a private trust company can provide to its
owners and third parties depends largely on the
jurisdiction where it is formed. Later in this chapter, we
will provide an overview of private trust companies as
well as a look at those specifically located in Switzerland,

*"It isn't enough to
have a trust fund
any more. The next
step is to have your
own trust company."*
-*Wall Street Journal*

Ireland and Caribbean jurisdictions newly-welcoming trust companies, all possessing their own unique advantages.

A Private Trust Company is similar to a Private International Bank

While a PTC differs greatly from an Asset Protection Trust, it is actually rather similar to a private international bank. Among the many applications of a private trust company, its owners will be afforded the ability to:

- Establish corresponding banking relationships to work directly with other banking institutions
- Monetize and collateralize assets and commodities
- Facilitate transactions on behalf of shareholders and clients without public record disclosure
- Provide ease of interaction with various international markets including ForEx trading
- Provide money management services including engaging in trust service activities and managing contracts for portfolio management.
- Accepting funds from investors to raise capital for international projects
- Issue financial instruments including Letters of Credit, Safe Keeping Receipts, Loans, and Promissory Notes to name a few
- Join prestigious international money exchanges such as SWIFT, Euroclear and Clearstream systems
- Process credit, debit, ACH and prepaid card services
- Legitimize the application of other international financial institutions (such as banks and insurance companies)

The small differences between a PTC and a bank come only in acts restricted to "banking" institutions. This includes offering interest earning cash deposits and writing bank guarantees. If you or your firm does not need these functions, a PTC may fulfill your needs to own a financial institution.

Major Benefits of a Private Trust Company

Owners of a private trust company are typically looking to accomplish two main goals, increasing profit and obtaining asset protection.

Profit

In today's competitive marketplace, there are only two methods of profit; cut costs or sell more. Owners of PTCs cut costs by carrying on fiduciary activities without the use of a third party. Additionally, owners expand their services by charging a premium to service third parties. For example, the company may issue letters of credit, hold commodities, process debit & credit cards and provide portfolio management and investment services to third parties.

> *"Wealth is the product of a man's capacity to think."*
> *-Ayn Rand*

One example of use of a private trust company to both cut costs and increase services is establishing credit, debit, ACH and prepaid card processing. Acquiring an international financial institution allows businesses, even those already engaged in processing, to network with a large number of international banks, giving the processor options for acquiring banks. These options lead to better contracts, reducing the total cost of processing. In addition, by contracting multiple international banks, limits on volume of processing can be hugely expanded if not eliminated all together. Many prominent third-party payment processors and large internet retailers are currently enjoying the benefits of bank networking through a private trust company.

Asset Protection

An individual or corporation does not need to have huge goals of profit when considering a private trust company; asset protection is a driving force in private trust company acquisition. Litigation in the United States has reached epic proportions, and, according to Forbes Magazine, is now a bigger threat to wealth than Taxes. A private trust company can provide asset protection by managing a shareholder's trust account with privacy and anonymity.

In terms of asset protection for individuals and families, a private trust company is the ultimate tool. Private trust companies can perform similar duties of an asset protection trust. However, as noted in an article in Forbes magazine regarding the benefits of private trust companies, "with a private trust company, the firm itself—not the individual officers or directors—is liable for any breach of fiduciary duty."[1] Additionally, the private trust company, by pooling family assets, is flexible enough to include those individual family members whose assets alone would not be large enough to form a separate trust or qualify for a hedge fund. In some cases, simply locating assets offshore is a major advantage in eliminating threat from lawsuit. Beyond this protection, some unique jurisdictions allow for ownership of private trust companies through bearer share certificates, making the company's owners anonymous.

Trust Companies Gaining Prevalence

The concept of PTCs has gained a heavy following amongst wealthy individuals and their families as a way of preserving their wealth and obtaining a larger say in their financial affairs. A top Beverly Hills, California attorney specializing in the estate planning field noted:

---

[1] Trust Yourself, Forbes, *www.forbes.com/forbes/1998/1012/6208062a_print.html*

"Wealthy families are taking more control over the inheritance process. One element that is gaining in popularity is the 'private trust company.' Rather than have the family's money under the control of institutions who often are more interested in selling a 'product' and providing good counsel, the families are turning inward."[2]

A recent Forbes Magazine article points out that some of the largest holders of private wealth in the world, including "the Bell family of General Mills, the Cargills of the grain-trading company, the Pratt family of Standard Oil (Pratt was Rockefeller's partner), and by members of the Ziff family whose core wealth is publishing," have all formed or acquired private trust companies.[3]

[2] Fisher, Howard S. *If You Really Want Control Your Wealth, Then Think SMALL!*
[3] *Trust Yourself,* <u>Forbes Online</u>

The Wall Street Journal further affirms the rise of private trust companies saying "It isn't enough to have a trust fund any more. The next step is to have your own trust company." The journal calls out the unique needs of some families and ultimately only trust companies being able to fulfill those needs:

> *"Families often turn to private trust companies if they have special assets, such as a closely held family business, real-estate or partnership interests, that they don't feel comfortable handing over to either an individual or a big trust company to manage or they want to ensure that the particular asset isn't sold."* [4]

Global Money Transfer through a Private Trust Company

A very select group of private trusts and fiduciary companies have established themselves as part of an elite group connected to the major financial transfer systems such as SWIFT, Euroclear and Clearstream. Through membership in these organizations, a relatively small, private financial organization can establish itself within the banking and securities system and affect a wire transfer or trade as quickly as Bank of America or Oppenheimer. SWIFT, which stands for Society for Worldwide Interbank Financial Telecommunication, is the most efficient method to send payment instructions between banks. The automated SWIFT system began to replace the old manual Telex some thirty years ago. Where Telex topped out at processing 10,000 transactions per day without timing guarantees, SWIFT currently exceeds eight million transactions daily with an average processing time of twenty seconds. The industry-owned cooperative supplies a secure, standardized messaging service and interface software to 7,500 financial institutions in 199 countries.

---

[4] Silverman, Rachel Emma. *Matters of Trust: Super-Rich Set Up Companies,* Wall Street Journal, August 4, 2007.

Clearstream and the more popular EuroClear are both securities settlement systems similar in design and operation to that of SWIFT. Euroclear is a Brussels-based organization while Clearstream is established in Luxembourg. These European clearing systems support over 2,500 different companies in eighty locations worldwide, primarily processing securities transactions, bonds, equities and investment funds traded in the Euromarkets. These institutions are so similar and coordinated that they are in the process of creating an automated daytime electronic communications link to facilitate quick settlement between the two.

The ability for a small institution to gain membership in these prestigious transfer systems does not mean that the floodgates are open and the "country club" has become public. It does mean, however, if you are a responsible, credible and seasoned financial institution from a highly regulated country, you may qualify. Joining the network of these clearinghouses is a huge coup for a smaller institution that is vying for respectability and credibility with its customers and international counterparts.

"In the business world, the rearview mirror is always clearer than the windshield."
Warren Buffett

Qualifying criteria for an "established" PTC to enter the systems is not completely defined. However, the minimum recommended age for the PTC is ten years, with assets exceeding $5 million USD. Local directors, with extensive banking and securities backgrounds are essential. In addition, close relationships with the banks and securities firms that will consider acting as your sponsor are imperative (just like your private country club...money isn't everything).

The timeframe to set up each system is approximately three months and will cost in excess of $75,000 USD (not including the hiring of operators for the 24 hour system). If you are seriously developing your financial organization, however, acceptance is a tremendous opportunity to gain control of your company's financial transactions, expedite your processing time, maintain business privacy and save money by reducing the service fees charged by larger institutions. Most importantly, you will gain prestige by being associated with the world leaders of your industry.

"Plans are nothing; planning is everything."
-Dwight D. Eisenhower

Choosing a Jurisdiction for a Private Trust Company

PTCs are available both domestically and internationally, though the benefits discussed in this chapter are generally reserved to those companies located abroad. The main consideration with jurisdiction is credibility. Beyond credibility of the jurisdiction, credibility of the company itself, i.e. newly formed or seasoned and established, is a major consideration. Lastly, and equally important, the regulations regarding restricted activities of the trust company garner consideration.

Swiss Trust Companies

Synonymous with the terms prestige, tradition and prosperity is the country of Switzerland, one of the most powerful financial centers in the world. The World Economic Forum's Global Competitiveness Report currently ranks Switzerland's economy as the most competitive in the world. When the credibility of the Swiss banking system is combined with experienced administration and the goodwill of an established STC, most major international banks, brokerages and insurance companies will welcome correspondent relationships, which are not easily formed on behalf of organizations established in jurisdictions of lesser quality and reputation.

Swiss law allows for the creation of new trust companies. However, those STCs established prior to the Swiss Code amendments of Feb. 1997 enjoy grandfather clauses that allow for the highest degree of privacy available in the market today. These seasoned STCs are rare opportunities, but offer the benefit of ownership through bearer share certificate.

"Wealth is not a matter of intelligence it's a matter of inspiration."
Jim Rohn

STCs are legal fiduciaries that provide their beneficial owners and clients ultimate control over their finances. A seasoned STC enjoys an unrestricted license, meaning the company can interact with a number of third parties by providing services such as portfolio management, insurance and real estate brokerage, holding of commodities and electronic payment processing. In some cases, an STC may even gain a Self-Regulating Organization license, allowing the clients of the STC to remain anonymous.

Irish Trust Companies

Due to excellent political and economic stability, a first-rate infrastructure, and a government that is investor and business-friendly, Ireland is an attractive jurisdiction for offshore private trust companies. As a developed nation with a well-regulated banking system, Ireland provides credibility to trust companies domiciled there. Often, Irish trust companies will be newly established rather than seasoned, reducing the overall credibility.

Irish Trusts are similar to Swiss Trusts in many regards; they are financial institutions with the authority to perform a wide-range of fiduciary and administrative functions to unrestricted third parties. Those functions may include opening correspondent bank accounts, obtaining membership in SWIFT, electronic payment processing and many others mentioned previously. If Ireland is a favorable jurisdiction for your business contacts, considering an acquisition in Ireland may suit your business plan.

Other Jurisdictions of Note

In recent years, many offshore jurisdictions that typically welcomed private banks have written legislation regarding the formation of private trust companies. The Bahamas, New Zealand, Costa Rica and Belize, to name a few, offer unique financial structures including private trust companies. There are two important factors that make these private trust companies wholly different than others discussed in the chapter: one, they will not garner comparable international prestige; two, they may have restrictions as to who the trust can do business with.

Take for example the British Virgin Islands which has recently gained popularity as a private trust company domicile. Primarily affecting the prestige of the organization, the reputation of Caribbean banking centers is not nearly as beneficial as European banking centers. Beyond this, while a seasoned trust company typically offers thirty years or more of marked operating history, a newly formed BVI trust company has no record of good business. International banks welcome interactions with established trusts; often, a particular trust will already have an operating history with a respected international bank. These same banks and possibly prestigious transfer systems like SWIFT will be reluctant to extend the same goodwill toward a newly formed company.

In addition to compromising prestige with a newly formed company, those individuals going to a location like the BVI should be aware of legislation regarding restricted business. A restricted license permits the trust company to only do business with named shareholders of the company; this structure may be suitable as an international holding company if the subsidiaries and trust plan on doing business internally rather than with other entities. The BVI in particular does offer unrestricted licenses for a paid in capital no less than $250,000; these licenses are preferable for businesses looking to gain positive interactions with external organization.

Conclusion

Private Trust Companies, either newly formed or longstanding, are a great alternative to private banks in that they provide unique opportunities to increase profit while obtaining asset protection. If your business model lends itself to a newly formed trust company, the acquisition may be less costly. With any offshore endeavor, remember: the entity is priced according to its value. Less costly companies tend to offer less value to their owners In recent years, Private Trust Companies have gained a significant following amongst wealthy individuals and their families looking to have more control over their assets and wealth. This trend will only continue to grow in the coming years.

Chapter 10

"The Evolution of Global Banking"

It used to be that nations with the highest GDP and most productive economies were the greatest banking centers. These nations, such as the United States, may have taken conservative stances regarding banking regulation and more specifically offshore banking. Today, isolationism is no longer an option for governments wishing to compete on an international basis, and economic globalization and the growth of rapid communications technology has had a huge impact on the growth of offshore markets. Relatively small nations with low GDP can compete on an international scale for the business of the world's wealthiest individuals and corporations. Domestic banks frequently seek out offshore markets that offer more substantial profit margins.

Twentieth Century Conservatism

The 1920's were characterized by wild speculation in the financial markets and the subsequent stock market crash of 1929 - the most famous crash in US history. The 1929 crash followed a bull market that had been running for the better part of a decade. In September of 1929, the Dow Jones Industrial Average hit a high of 386; that same level would not be seen again until 1954, some twenty-five years later. Many reasons have been given for the downfall; top among them is the reckless commingling of funds between US banks and the brokerage houses they owned. These excesses were the catalyst to legislative changes initiated by President Franklin D. Roosevelt in the wake of the Great Depression.

The primary banking legislation following the crash came in the form of the Glass-Steagall Banking Act of 1933 - enacted to regulate problematic activities by separating banking from the securities business. This separation was very strict until the 1980's when US commercial banks were in a new marketplace and at an extreme disadvantage. Most notably, securities firms were offering money market instruments that gave instant liquidity and higher rates of return to investors. Once the securities firms captured their new clients, cross selling other products and services became rather easy to do. US banks were increasingly less competitive, and the wealth of many of America's wealthiest was being held by securities firms or perhaps offshore.

"Toleration and liberty are the foundations of a great republic."
- Frank Lloyd Wright

In 1984, the "Fed" allowed a commercial bank to purchase a discount brokerage house. In an attempt to protect market share, the Securities Industry Association challenged this action under the premise that it was a direct violation of Glass-Steagall. The Supreme Court however, ruled in favor of the Federal Reserve Board's action. This opened the door for numerous other commercial banking institutions to petition for similar ownership; the result being the evolution of entities that came to be known as "Section 20" subsidiaries. Over the years the authority of these entities was expanded to encompass activities previously excluded. Section 20's provided the first major example that conservative stances toward banking regulation would sacrifice the competitive edge of US banks, and the future may hold less regulation.

Eventually, the provision providing for Section 20's was antiquated when the Clinton Administration repealed the Glass-Steagall Banking Act and created the Gramm-Leach-Bliley Act. Again pointing to the trend of financial deregulation, the law that had once banned brokerages and banks from joining together was replaced by one that allowed for more flexibility. Large conglomerates like Citigroup, formed by the merger of Citibank with Travelers Group, served as both banking and trading superpowers. The Gramm-Leach-Bliley Act also amended the Bank Holding Company Act to permit affiliations among financial services companies, including banks, securities firms and insurance companies.

Financial modernization in the United States was inevitable as the internet, effective international travel, and business globalization offered countless options for universal banking. The deregulation of US banks points to the boldest trend that would take hold in the first years of twenty-first century – a world marketplace. Even as the great crashes of the housing and global credit markets in 2007 and 2008 point out deficiencies in the deregulation of markets in the 90s, it is evident that the solution can not be to adopt a conservative-isolationist stance. A plethora of external factors now affect each participant in global marketplace, and large players like the US compete daily for business with diverse nations.

A Global Economy Leads to Global Banking

An example in US banking history of changing viewpoints rests in the US definition of Trust Companies. In the early 19th century, the American Trust Company was introduced when small corporations began performing trust functions closely similar to banking functions. In New York State, "the words 'Trust Company' had come to encompass activities very different from those previously understood in Anglo-Saxon law. Collateral received as security for loans was understood to be taken in trust, and trust companies became, in effect, lenders on collateral." Trust Companies and banks were largely separate, and banks were not permitted from acting as trusts or even writing mortgages, often making them less competitive than trusts. By the early 20th century, Trust Companies were the dominant financial institutions as they enjoyed more flexibility than even state or federally chartered banks. Today, even though constantly changing regulations have drawn lines between the powers of banks, trusts and securities brokers, New York carries the history of its powerful trust companies as "three of New York's seven giant banks -Morgan Guaranty, Bankers and Irving - are by name Trust Companies."[1] Just as trust company powers and banking powers have changed constantly in US history, viewpoints and regulation regarding the authority of offshore banks have seen dramatic shifts.

"I believe totally in a capitalist system, I only wish that someone would try it."
- Frank Lloyd Wright

It is clear, that perspectives on offshore banking have dramatically changed as it has evolved into a common place business endeavor for individuals as well as corporations. For nearly two decades now, offshore banking has been in the midst of such a transition.

In the past 50 years, the growth in the offshore banking marketplace has been unparalleled. As recently as the 1960s, "Offshore banking was almost exclusively controlled by the Swiss ... Such countries as the Channel Islands and Cayman Islands then followed."[2] Their success resulted in other jurisdictions, short on natural resources and domestic economic growth, to look at this emerging marketplace as a viable industry. Offshore Banking now includes virtually all of the world's financial markets.

Recent estimates have the approximate annual growth of the offshore banking sector at 15% per annum. Many feel that

---

[1] Martin Mayer, "The Bankers" Weybright & Talley, p.488
[2] "Offshore Outlook", Gins Globe Communications

this number is way too conservative. Recent International Monetary Fund (IMF) statistics indicate that, "of the leading 12 international banking centers, ranked by foreign deposits, six can be tightly defined as offshore centers."[3] Such statistics however, can be misleading. As previously noted, all free countries offer foreign investment incentive, ultimately meaning all free countries, including highly taxed markets such as the US, compete as tax havens for foreign citizens.

The New Major Players in Offshore Banking

The four largest offshore jurisdictions in terms of bank deposits are: the Cayman Islands, the Grand Duchy of Luxembourg, Hong Kong and Switzerland. These are closely followed by Singapore and the Bahamas. Although these nations are not centers of any industry other than financial services, the top four nations have a GDP estimated to be in the top ten in the world, pointing to the large scope of the offshore banking arenas they host.

Cayman Islands

Located in the western Caribbean, just a short distance from Jamaica, this tiny nation with a population of 32,000 has become the fifth largest banking center in the World, exceeded only by Japan, the United Kingdom, France and the United States. The three Islands of Grand Cayman, Cayman Brac and Little Cayman were a dependency of Jamaica until 1959, and, since that time, they have been a territory of Great Britain. Their economy is sustained by offshore services, business services and tourism.

Contrary to popular myth, the Caymans have developed strict guidelines for conducting banking business. Strong anti-money laundering measures have been put in place

---

[3] Ibid

including the signing of the mutual legal assistance treaty in association with the United States and the United Kingdom; these regulatory improvements have enhanced the international standing of the island nation. The Caymans are also a member of the Caribbean Financial Action Task Force, an organization that will share information under specific circumstances.

Of the world's top fifty banks, forty have subsidiaries here; this fact alone indicates the Caymans importance. There are currently over 560 banks and trust companies licensed to carry on business from the Caymans. Within that figure, over sixty different countries are represented. The estimated totals for bank deposits exceed 520 billion US dollars.

The major names that one would find here include:

- Bank of Bermuda
- Bank of Butterfield
- Barclays
- Royal Bank of Canada
- Bank of America
- Scotia Bank
- JPMorgan Chase
- Coutts & Co. Ltd.
- Goldman Sachs
- Midland Bank Trust Corporation
- Merrill Lynch Bank & Trust

The Cayman Islands has been able to separate itself from other emerging offshore centers by the caliber of its financial infrastructure. In addition to housing numerous law firms knowledgeable in global finance and taxation, the Cayman Islands hosts offices to all of the world's major accounting firms. Furthermore, because the Caymans act as a major insurance center, sophisticated management firms provide insurance coverage for foreign and domestic firms. Despite the goodwill of many major international regulatory boards, anyone considering doing business here must consider the potential for negative preconceptions. To this day, in the eyes of many, the Caymans still struggle with an image problem.

Luxembourg

Located in the heart of the European Economic Community, Luxembourg's legislation is among the most liberal in Europe and stands firmly behind stringent bank secrecy laws. Written history of Luxembourg actually begins in the year 963 when Sigefroid, count of the Ardennes, founded the Luxembourg Dynasty. Today, this modest nation with a population of only 400,000 has parlayed itself into the fourth largest banking center in the world. Its economy is heavily oriented to the markets of neighboring countries with exports accounting for 80% of the nation's production.

"It can actually be stated that Germany's most dynamic and profitable financial center is not in Germany, its in the neighboring Grand Duchy of Luxembourg. During the period from 1986 to 1994, the number of German Banks more than doubled. Germans have deposited almost as much money into Grand Duchy's investment funds as in their own country. The mass exodus of money started when the German government slapped a 10% withholding tax on investment income. Although the tax was scrapped after only six months, the flow of money had started and would not soon stop. While difficult to measure, bankers estimate the net capital flow to Luxembourg from Germany to be at $77 billion, or approximately 4% of Germany's gross national product."[4]

International banks found their way to Luxembourg in earnest during the 1960's, primarily to profit from the Euro market and this country's lower minimum reserves. There are now more than 130 international banks located here that include branches from many major nations such as the United States, United Kingdom, Germany, Belgium and Russia. "Luxembourg bankers employ over 20,000 while accounting for one-third of total government revenue by corporate and employee income taxes."[5]

The beauty and wealth of this scenic nation combined with generous business incentives offers considerable attraction to those desiring a European presence. Most Luxembourgers are only fluent in French and German; English is a third language and this can be a significant deterrent. In any case, this small country remains another shining example of the dramatic and positive growth provided by offshore banking.

---

[4] PeterGumbel, "Wall Street Journal", p.A31, 11/16/94
[5] "Offshore Outlook" Gins Globe Communications

Hong Kong

Hong Kong enjoys a strategic location in East Asia, bordering the South China Sea and China. China formally ceded control of Hong Kong in 1842 when Hong Kong was occupied by the UK. China and the UK later agreed to Hong Kong's official status as the Hong Kong Special Administrative Region (SAR) of China in 1997. The famous "one country, two systems" formula China devised, whereby Hong Kong would not be submitted to China's socialist economic system, allowed Hong Kong to benefit from autonomy in all economic concerns.

Hong Kong is highly dependent on international trade. As recently as 2006, "the total value of goods and services trade, including the sizable share of reexports, was equivalent to 400% of GDP."[6] Mainland China has taken a larger role in the economy of Hong Kong in recent years, including being the most sizable trading partner, making up almost half of total trade.

---

[6] CIA World Factbook, 2008

Once an industry giant, Hong Kong's manufacturing industry has largely left the prosperous autonomous region for mainland China, and Hong Kong has become a primarily service-oriented economy. As a premier exchange, the Hong Kong Stock Exchange lists many Chinese companies seeking global markets. The exchange is now only behind Shanghai and Tokyo in terms of major Asian exchanges, and Hong Kong is largely recognized as an economic center throughout not just Asia but the world market. While many fear that China will eventually seek total control of Hong Kong, it remains an attractive destination for many mainlanders seeking offshore benefits, and it is attractive to global entrepreneurs who are looking to capitalize on its autonomous status.

Switzerland

Since gaining independence from the Holy Roman Empire in 1499, The Swiss Confederation has enjoyed an honorable tradition of and reputation for autonomy and neutrality. One of the few European countries not involved in either major World War, Switzerland has since strengthened its ties with the rest or Europe and the UN in the past fifty years. Although Switzerland is not a member of the UN, officially obtaining membership in 2002, the nation still shows a fervent pledge to neutrality, especially in its banking systems.

Among the many attractive features drawing international banks to Switzerland, the low unemployment rate, a "highly skilled labor force, and a per capita GDP larger than that of the big Western European economies" make Switzerland a stronghold in the world economy.[7] To compete in the global marketplace, even the Swiss have conformed with the EU's economic standards. Switzerland is unique

---

[7] CIA World Factbook, 2008

because it has been able to accomplish this conformity without compromising the bank secrecy that has made it a financial superpower and maintained the Swiss franc's notorious market power.

Singapore

Quickly becoming one of the hubs of Asia's banking market, the island state of Singapore offers an exemplary safe haven. The Republic of Singapore is situated north of the equator at the southeastern end of the Strait of Malacca. Independence from Malaysia was gained in 1965. With a population of almost three million, the vast majority being of Chinese ancestry, nationals in Singapore are known as Singaporeans. The official languages include; Chinese, Malay, Tamil and English. Immigration grants to live in Singapore are dispensed on a highly selective basis, primarily due to the moderate capacity of available land. Historically, Singapore represents the site of one of the greatest military defeats in British history that took place on February 15, 1942 when 80,000 British troops surrendered to the Japanese.

"Of all the financial institutions domiciled in Singapore, 129 commercial banks are in operation including 13 local institutions. The remaining 116 foreign banks have 22 full banking licenses, 14 restricted banking licenses and 80 offshore banking licenses. Banks with offshore licenses deal mainly in the Asian dollar; foreign exchange transactions and their activities are mostly centered on the wholesale banking business of non-residents."[8]

The development of Singapore as an international financial center continues to be a major policy objective for its government. Financial institutions operating here represent a diverse range of potential products and services. In order to encourage multinational corporations to headquarter their operations in Singapore, numerous government tax and investment incentives exist. The appeal of Singapore rests in its ability to be well regulated yet financially sound; the 1988 crisis of bad debt did not create economic woes in Singapore as it did for many other Asian countries.

The Bahamas

As explored in previous chapters, the Bahamas represent a highly desirable nation for both individuals and corporations looking to conduct international business. Its proximity to the United States combined with its white sands and turquoise colored surf has made it one of North America's favorite tourist destinations. Tourism accounts for nearly 40% of this country's gross national product by annually contributing an estimated US $1.2 billion. The local population is approximately 273,000 with the official language being English. Their currency is the Bahamian dollar which is pegged to the US dollar on a 1:1 ratio.

---

[8] "The Investor's Guide to Singapore", p.22

The Bahamas have a long-standing and uninterrupted democratic legacy. Since 1729, their political system has been based on the British style of parliamentarian government. Quickly approaching three hundred years of democratic rule, this nation of islands can now lay claim to be one of the most stable countries in the world. In 1973, The Bahamas became fully independent and a member of the United Nations.

Many of the world's largest financial institutions have taken advantage of this unwavering political environment. Currently, over four hundred banks from thirty-six different countries are licensed to do business within or from The Bahamas. This in conjunction with their vehement protection of personal privacy has positioned this small country to be a major force in offshore banking.

Conclusion

These examples of relatively small nations becoming great financial centers shows that banks, corporations and individuals will take their money and their business to those markets that offer more substantial profit margins and the greatest benefits. International competition means that relatively small nations with low industry or little natural resources can compete with previous superpowers. Those superpowers, such as the United States and China, cannot effectively opt for isolationism in the wake of economic globalization. Isolationist, conservative stances toward offshore banking are outdated, as evidenced by its explosive growth in the past 50 years. Even as forces like the UN or the FATF push for greater regulation and universal standards, smaller nations with traditions of bank privacy will still enjoy less regulatory oversight than major super powers. Offshore business, like any technically sound business model, is here to stay.

"Be curious, not judgmental."
-Walt Whitman

Chapter 11

"Profit"

Nearly every individual or business that enters into private bank ownership does so with one of three intentions: Profit, Privacy or Asset Protection. In the following chapters, we will provide a detailed overview of each of these three intentions specifically noting how each is easily obtained through ownership of a private financial institution. Again, as we have continued to reiterate throughout this book, it is essential to seek the advice of a professional prior to "going offshore."

Profit

Webster's Dictionary defines profit as *"the compensation accruing to entrepreneurs for the assumption of risk in a business enterprise"*. More specifically, profit is the positive gain from an investment or business operation after subtracting for all expenses. The bottom line for every new business endeavor is to make a profit; Private International Bank ownership is no different. The ability to generate enormous profits, perhaps the largest percentages available to any entrepreneur, is one of the major attributes of this industry.

Private International Banking brings high-net-worth individuals a full range of customized private banking services, global investment opportunities and superior advice. The extent to which a PIB owner can provide these services is directly equivalent to the level of his bank's profitability. An affluent client's financial success creates

" No profit grows where there is no pleasure taken."
– William Shakespeare

the need for specialized banking and investment services. Since no two individuals' finances are identical, they require expertise not normally available at most large institutions. This need for specialized service opens the door for a highly unique niche-market. Therefore, to be profitable, the primary focus of a PIB should be wealth preservation, wealth enhancement and personalized service.

There are three major aspects to be considered that pertain to profit:
1) Operating expenditures
2) Specific banking services to offer potential clients
3) Specific products that might be sold to potential clients

It must be noted that no list of business options can be all encompassing. There will always be additional ways a bank can profit based upon the owner's background, personal associations and industry expertise. We will, however, endeavor to present a synopsis of ideas that will point to a few areas not readily apparent.

Lower Expenditures, Higher Profit Margins

In terms of bottom line gains, "nothing else a bank can do will add so quickly or so substantially to its profits as a reduction in the overall cost of operations."[1] An offshore bank offers an entrepreneur the opportunity to profit from his or her efforts and expertise with an extremely low outlay of capital. When compared with its domestic alternative, expenditures are often at a rate of one fiftieth the required capital. Even during the initial acquisition phase, which is typically the most expensive, costs can be readily kept to a minimum. Numerous other expenses, however, may come into play. Management, administration, marketing, accounting, regulation and system controls are a few of the

---

[1] Martin Mayer, "The Bankers" Weybright & Talley, p.156

general areas that, if left unchecked, could affect profit margins. Here, too, exists a low-cost solution that will enable an owner to accomplish these needed tasks without a huge outlay of cash.

Profits will always be the measure of a PIB's success, and, as such, they should offer maximum margins. Owning and operating a private offshore banking entity can be cost efficient, flexible and uncomplicated. An offshore banking entity will not have the "storefront" appearance that might normally be associated with domestic financial institutions. Gone are the marquees, teller lines, vaults and other retail administrative aspects, as well as, the expenses related to such items. The PIB uses clearing accounts with major international banking institutions for physical deposits and independent offshore administrative firms for all other functions. In this manner, the owner is able to leverage time, meet fiduciary responsibilities and transact business while keeping expenditures to a minimum. As a result, the profit margin is much greater offshore.

"There are always opportunities through which businessmen can profit handsomely if they will only recognize and seize them."

– Jean Paul Getty

The management and administration of a PIB should be conducted offshore, outside the owner's country of residence, with great care taken to ensure that deposit taking activities do not breach domestic banking laws. Few things have a greater impact on the degree of success for a PIB than quality management service. Since owners usually have little banking or international administrative experience, they rely on the management company to perform key administrative functions for them, as well as contribute invaluable advice. For a surprisingly low fee, a top-notch management firm can process deposits, handle mail, telephone and facsimile communications as well as keeping track of receipts. Additionally, they can maintain an office enabling them to provide typing, photocopying, filing and "piggy-backing" their reputation and international banking relationships onto a newly formed entity. The average owner will spend between $2,500 to $5,000 per year for basic administrative assistance, which is significantly much less than the cost of one good employee. Should expenditures exceed this range, the bank would have to be extremely active, a likely indicator of success.

After the entity has been properly structured, it is essential to expedite the necessary introductions to facilitate the required professional, international associations. We recommend working with a reputable firm that has qualified, global relationships with numerous offshore management firms. Locations such as Hong Kong, Switzerland, France, Belgium and England are just some of the host countries where these businesses are domiciled.

Offshore Management Services
(Representative Quotes providing a typical range of costs)

1)   Hourly service for assisting in company banking practices that require review by Director, and/or legal advice. US$60 - US$150 per man-hour
2)   Hourly service for filing and accounting functions. US$50 - US$60 per man-hour
3)   Opening bank accounts for the corporation and their clients. US$110 per account or US$50 - US$80 per man-hour
4)   If necessary, establishing dedicated phone and facsimile lines for the company. US$150 per line
5)   If necessary, hiring a private secretary.
     Three separate options:
     a) US$1,800 per month, including desk and office

b) US$80 per man-hour
c) US$12,000 Average cost per annum
d) Minimum retainer desired, if any.
   US$1,500 - US$3,000

Services to Offer

One of the first and most important questions any entrepreneur should ask of themselves is, "What type of bank do we want to be?" As previously discussed, complex financial needs of successful individuals and multinational corporations requires increased specialization. To avoid the pitfalls of trying to be all things to all people, the owner should be willing to target a specific, niche market. The following provides a glance at various services to present.

Services to Wealthy Individuals

Everyone markets to the wealthy yet few truly do so in a successful manner. The key is not only to offer an important service but to be seen as different from competitors. The ability to stand out from the crowd is the difference between success and failure. Few vehicles can make your operation more unique than owning an offshore financial institution. Services that may be found the most attractive would include:

- Confidential & Numbered Accounts
- Precious Coin Trading & Services
- International Credit Cards
- International Brokerage Services
- Trust Services
- Arbitrage & Currency Activities
- Precious Gem Trading & Services
- Offshore Portfolio Management
- Commodities Brokerage

Services to Multinational Corporations

Multinational corporations often have a multitude of unique needs that avoid precise definition. By offering services that larger banks find too cumbersome, a profitable business can be pursued. The range of needed services would be very broad and technical and may include:

- Investment Banking
- Venture Capital
- International Loans
- Knowledge of Exchange Controls
- Offshore Labor Information
- Offshore Associations with Major Banks
- Access to International Mutual Funds
- Correspondent banking relationships
- Credit Card Processing

"An idealist is one who helps the other fellow to make a profit."
– Henry Ford

Accounts & Products to Sell

When a bank owner takes in a deposit it is considered a liability. The balance sheet will reflect it as such since there exists a fiduciary responsibility to repay that sum of money, in addition to the agreed upon interest rate. The client is essentially loaning their funds to the bank. The bank looks to profit from the spread between the repayment costs and the return that can be generated. The term "bank account" relates to deposits taken in by the bank, yet products are usually packaged outside investments. In either case, a number of distinct advantages exist over domestic institutions because of the lack of regulatory restrictions and expenses. Some of the accounts and products that can be sold to a client would include the following as listed below.

1. Current Accounts

The most common type of foreign bank account, this offers clients the highest degree of flexibility. It allows withdrawal of all or part of the account balance at any time and can have check writing privileges. Most current accounts pay interest, and offer deposit or withdrawal of funds in the client's choice of currencies.

(From our perspective, this type of account offers the owner the most expense and headaches. It is most often associated with "A" Class banking operations.)

2. Deposit Accounts

Simply stated, a deposit account is a savings account in a foreign country. The account pays interest but the rate of return varies according to the currency in which the account is denominated and the length of time for which the money is deposited. Generally, the longer the money is held, the higher the interest rate. Most deposit accounts require a minimum of US$5,000. Certain restrictions can be placed on withdrawals.

(This account is more attractive for the owner to offer because of greater profit potential. The spread between the interest rate guaranteed the investor and where the funds might be reinvested by the bank is typically 5-10%. For example, a US$25,000 investment by your client could result in a US$1,250 to US$2,500 profit.)

3. Numbered Accounts

A numbered account is an account identified by a number rather than by a name, and, to that extent, it provides a certain amount of privacy and protection. In the past, Switzerland, Belgium, Luxembourg and Mexico have all offered this banking service.

(A very marketable service when used in connection with an attractive interest rate.)

4. Managed Accounts

Managed accounts are reserved for larger depositors. The typical account minimum starts at US$500,000 but could be as much as US$10,000,000. With this account, the client chooses to use the bank's investment advisors to manage their portfolio consisting of written, established investment goals. Managed accounts are offered for stocks, currencies, bonds, commodities, limited partnerships or a combination. The bank charges a fee for this service based on a percentage of funds under management. In addition, a nominal annual fee is charged ranging from US$40 to US$100. Offering managed accounts can be a very profitable service, if the bank owner can bring new clients to the table. This usually results in a fee sharing arrangement between the bank and the manager. The profit from just one large account could amount to thousands of dollars per year.

5. Letters of Credit (LOC or L/C)

In its most common form, a Letter of Credit is a bank's conditional undertaking of payment. Expressed more fully, a letter of credit is a conditional commitment by the issuing bank to pay money to a seller of goods (beneficiary), on behalf of the buyer (applicant). The applicant initiates this transaction and agrees to pay at sight or within a specified time limit against documents. The conditions upon which the bank's obligation will be invoked are specified in the L/C. To ensure uniformity of interpretation in international trade, the International Chamber of Commerce has established a set of regulations pertaining to Letters of Credit entitled "Uniform Customs and Practice for Documentary Credits".

LOCs consist of at least five elements:

a. **CONSIDERATION** - to the bank for issuance of an L/C. The bank charges a fee or commission for issuing or opening the L/C.

b. **EXPIRY DATE** - of the L/C must be stated in the body of the instrument.

c. **MAXIMUM AMOUNT** - of the bank's obligations is stated in the L/C.

d. **ISSUING BANK'S OBLIGATION TO PAY** - supersedes that of the buyer. In other words, once the bank issues an L/C it is obligated to the beneficiary.

e. **ACCOUNT PARTY IS OBLIGATED** - in an enforceable written agreement to reimburse the bank for payments made in accordance with the agreement. The bank's credit risk is therefore with the applicant of the L/C.

(Another potential source of profit for the Bank is the ability to issue LOCs. Marketing potential is excellent. The import and export industry typically tends to be in need of this service. An offshore bank could take advantage of this cash flow between the two parties by offering the same service as a larger institution at a reduced cost. The use of a good international administrative firm would become a necessity with this type of transaction.)

6. Other Lending Services

The Bank may also participate in various other lending activities including: Bank Guarantees, Secured Lending, Back-to-Back loans, Mortgages and more. It is very important that any loan agreement, especially those that might directly or indirectly involve a principal of the bank, be reviewed by a qualified legal professional.

(Lending services can be extremely profitable. Venture Capital loans at high interest rates are one of the most common activities.)

7. Certificates of Deposit

According to Federal Reserve Board statistics, foreign deposits of U.S. dollars totaled more that US$1 trillion at the end of 1989. A significant portion of these deposits were negotiable certificates of deposit issued by international banks. Your bank may be in a position to enter into the Eurodollar market and place its own CDs directly into the marketplace. The Eurodollar is a deposit in a bank outside the United States or in an International Banking Facility located in the United States (Permitted since 1981). The majority of Eurodollar deposits are still found outside the US, primarily in London based banks, where there is an active secondary market. The Eurodollar market is virtually unregulated. CDs are typically sold in bearer form in denominations of US$10,000 or more for periods of six months to 10 years.

(The long term time commitment associated with CDs provides an excellent profit opportunity for the Bank Owner. Reinvestment into real estate is very common.)

8. High Interest Loans

Venture capital loans offered at high interest rates are frequently utilized by Private International Banks. An important legal precedent was established by the California Courts in Sodeno v. Union Commerce Bank, 17 Cal.App.3d 391, 139 Cal. Rptr. 229 (1977), which held that foreign banks were exempt from California usury laws. Because of such court rulings, a PIB owner may in fact find themselves in certain business situations without competition.

Additional products & services that could be considered would include: International Credit Cards, International Mutual Funds and Secured Loans.

Case Study

The following scenario presents a real-life example of a client group who used private bank ownership to expand their business. As with many investment groups who own Private Banks, this group utilized the services to better manage and facilitate their existing investor base while offering new services to greatly increase their investor network. This case study serves to show a general representation of the profit potential available to owners of a private financial institution, but it is not representative of all the benefits & services available through various offshore institutions.

Please view Figure 1 on the following page.

Figure 1

Case Study:

Prospects Name:	Withheld
Industry:	Owner/Real Estate Developer
Company Name:	Withheld
Company Website:	Withheld
In Business Since:	Withheld

Need:
Profit / Preserve Opportunity / Privacy
Looking to raise capital from private investors
offering CD's, then issuing bank
guarantees to secure property for development.

Solution:
St. Vincent Bank with correspondent
account at National Commercial
Bank of St. Vincent and UBS.

Benefit:
Private Bank will create new opportunities to gain
profit from investors while ultimately helping its
owners to capitalize on opportunities by controlling
the movement of funds more efficiently.

Final Comments:
The client was able to accomplish his needs through ownership of a
captive bank in St. Vincent. The ability to raise capital from private
investors offering CD's was successfully met while increasing the
anonymity of their investments. Additionally, correspondent banking
relationships were created and afforded the owner the ability to
control the movement of funds quicker and more efficiently to
capitalize on new business opportunities.

WORLDWIDE BUSINESS CONSULTANTS. *Innovative Offshore Solutions Since 1991.*

Peripheral Services

1. Offshore Annuities

The Swiss insurance industry has become very popular by successfully marketing tax-free annuities. Swiss annuities typically require a minimum investment of US$10,000 which represents a substantial reduction from previous levels. In light of this success, the Private International Bank owner may want to consider expanding into this market. This may require the establishment of an international insurance company.

2. Offshore Mutual Funds

In the U.S. market alone, more than 1.6 trillion dollars is invested in domestic mutual funds. Each day another 1 million dollars gets placed in this area of investment with 28% of all households having ownership. Currently, 3,662 domestic mutual funds are now in business, predominately comprised of portfolios with stocks, bonds or a mixture of both. Exact numbers are difficult to obtain offshore due to the privacy element. However, it is fair to assume that this is also a huge marketplace and therefore, numerous opportunities exist. For example, option and commodity transactions are closely scrutinized domestically for the benefit of the investor. This is an excellent method for protecting the uninformed investor because of the inherent risk, but there are those that wish to participate in a diversified portfolio of these securities and this opens the door for those willing to manage such risk. Other areas also become a possibility such as oil, natural gas, arbitrage, real estate and rental properties to name a few. Finally, projects that may have an exotic objective can also be accomplished offshore. This would include interests in professional tennis players, golfers, entertainers, race horses and even the recovery of sunken treasure. By any measure, mutual fund

"Life is divided into three terms - that which was, which is, and which will be. Let us learn from the past to profit by the present, and from the present to live better in the future."

– William Wadsworth

growth over the last twenty years has been stunning. Consumers flock to mutual funds because of their low fees, professional management, positive press and ease of understanding. In the United States, domestic banks are barred from distributing mutual funds directly under the Glass-Steagall Act. That does not stop their interests from growing in this marketplace via sister companies and third-party marketers. These vendors act as a partner with the bank providing crucial administrative functions and distribution services. U.S. domestic banks are in this marketplace because of profit and it may be worth your serious consideration to pursue similar interests offshore. This strategy could require the establishment of an offshore fund.

Conclusion:

PIB Ownership is less expensive to establish and operate so the profit potential is substantially greater than any domestic alternative. The ability to provide highly specialized services to wealthy individuals further increases the overall profit potential of private bank owners. Varying by jurisdiction, there are many services that private banks can provide to their clients, all with varying administrative and operational costs. The most important consideration to take into effect is deciding what type of banking entity to be and ultimately structuring your private bank to directly reflect that consideration. Again, as always stated, it is essential to seek guidance from a professional expert in this industry prior to engaging in private bank ownership.

Chapter 12

"Asset Protection"

A fascinating piece of writing recently appeared in Forbes Magazine with the premise that litigation is actually a much greater threat to American wealth than taxes. According to the article, this is due to American citizens being exposed to an infinite amount of liability through an overworked system of litigation. Thus, high-net worth individuals are putting "unlimited assets" at risk. This article goes on to state that "contrary to the popular vision of offshore banking, the true purpose of these accounts for many wealthy clients is to protect a lifetime of earnings and savings not from being taxed, but from being wiped out in a major lawsuit--say, a medical malpractice or a class-action securities litigation against an executive."

Consider the following:

- *"Suing for damages has become both a huge industry and a tremendous drag on American industry's ability to compete."* - Forbes Magazine

- *"Plastic surgeons are being named in numerous lawsuits. One Texas malpractice insurer states that current premiums are running between US $20,000 - 80,000 and will likely jump 20% again."* - The Economist

- *"Every year in America individuals and businesses spend more than $80 billion on direct litigation costs and higher insurance premiums. When indirect costs are included, the costs may add up to a figure in excess of $300 billion."* - President's Council on Competitiveness

Potential Sources of Lawsuits

1. Divorce
2. Employee actions or employee termination
3. Guest accidents at home
4. Rental or industrial property ownership
5. Actions of business associates
6. Service as a corporate director
7. Volunteerism
8. Advisory board member
9. Actions of your spouse or children
10. Product liability, safety or warranty

You will get Sued!!!

Reaching epidemic proportions, statistics now show that US citizens have a one in four chance of being sued during their lifetime. Business owners and professionals are the most likely to be sued; also included in that union are physicians, plastic surgeons, stockbrokers, law enforcement officials and real estate developers. Governing rules of civil procedures have been liberalized, consequentially making the process of taking legal action much easier than ever before. Results can be devastating, and products such as liability insurance are rarely enough to cover all eventualities. Traditional approaches to asset protection, such as utilizing a corporate veil to limit shareholder liability, are likewise seldom good enough. For instance, most liability insurance policies do not cover some of the most common reasons for civil litigation. Frequently excluded are: sexual harassment, wrongful termination, negligence or any type of punitive damages. In addition, policy limits are often severely under the multimillion dollar judgments being handed down. As a result, the use of offshore vehicles has been brought to the forefront of estate and financial planning.

Litigation has become a menacing economic weight. Testimonials can be supplied by anyone unfortunate enough to have gone through the process. Throughout the course of litigating a civil procedure, economic factors remain most important; issues of innocence or fault seem to have become lost within the system. Ultimately, a system remains where the bottom line is to find those holding the cash. As stated by one US state Supreme Court Judge, "As long as I am allowed to redistribute wealth from out-of-state companies to injured in-state plaintiffs, I shall continue to do so. Not only is my sleep enhanced when I give someone else's money away, but so is my job security, because in-state plaintiffs, their families and their friends will re-elect me." [1]

In modern society, it is now commonplace for plaintiffs to ignore those perceived to be of meager financial resources and sue the deepest pockets. Strategies have evolved for plaintiffs to find and attack this wealth. One example of a legal tactic frequently employed resembles guerrilla warfare, in which one side makes it too expensive for the other to continue the fight. The goal is to receive a substantial out of court settlement without ever coming close to going to trial.

"It has become much easier to sue someone today than it was thirty years ago. One of the most significant changes involved the adoption of something called 'notice pleading'. Notice pleading means that if a complaint contains satisfactory information to put the defendant on notice in a broad and very general nature of the allegations that are being made, the pleading is sufficient. In other words, the case will be heard. In days past, lawsuits had to be worded very specifically in order to survive. The rules

---

[1] Dr. Larry Turpen, "How & Why Americans Go Offshore", p.119

required something called issue pleading, which meant that in its initial complaint, the plaintiff in a lawsuit carried the burden of identifying the issues and advising the defendant of a large number of the facts involved in the claim. A wide array of technical requirements had to be met in order for the lawsuit to remain in court. Failure to meet those specific and demanding requirements often resulted in lawsuits being thrown out of court on what would now be called technical errors."[2]

The trend is ominous. Not only are liability insurance premiums dramatically moving upward, but now litigation takes longer to resolve. According to a recent study, the average number of months that individuals would need to engage a legal defense was fifty-one months. In addition, the average judgment was more than $1.5 million.

The cost of liability insurance has skyrocketed to the point of being nonsensical. "As early as 1984, London reinsurers labeled the US liability market uninsurable and started a mass exodus. By 1985 Lloyd's, the world's biggest reinsurer was scrambling to get out. It declared that the liability insurance scene in the US has lost all predictability and therefore has become impossible to assess in terms of premium rates. Another English underwriter stated that America was as unpredictable from an insurance point of view as a banana republic."[3]

Prolonged disputes have become the norm pointing to the inefficiencies of the present system. For example, medical malpractice and product liability cases follow a similar scenario. 1) Liability turning on very complicated fact situations, almost always calling for expensive expert witnesses, 2) litigation so expensive that only the largest

---

[2] Kenneth Menendez, "Taming the Lawyers", p.32
[3] Peter W. Huber, "Liability, The legal revolution and its consequences", p.141

claims are brought, 3) relatively little of the total loss being paid from liability insurance, 4) defendants winning approximately three-quarters of the cases that reach a verdict, 5) rapidly rising claims and premiums, and 6) most of the money going to lawyers and insurance companies rather than to accident victims.[4]

Virtually all aspects of our society are affected. More than three-quarters of all obstetricians and gynecologists have been hit with malpractice suits. As reported in the "The Detroit News", medical malpractice costs in such states as California, Florida and Michigan customarily have escalated to a minimal range of $125,000 to $185,000 per year, per physician. Likewise, plastic surgeons have numerous horror stories to add that specifically relate to the legal feeding frenzy surrounding silicone breast implants. Nearly all practicing physicians currently find or will discover themselves to be targets.

Class action suits are common place in many industries. The brokerage business has been particularly hard hit in recent years. One of the most noteworthy civil litigation filings indigenous to this industry was regarding Prudential Securities and limited partnerships it sold.

The Corporate Veil

For years, the traditional approach to asset protection had been to utilize the corporation. A corporation is typically seen and understood for legal purposes as a separate being. It limits shareholder liability to their investment in the corporation. This would provide a "veil" between the assets of the business and those of the shareholders. Until recently, this was often enough to protect principals from civil litigation.

---

[4] J. O'Connell, "Ending Insult to Injury", p.29

Too often, however, the US courts have shown a willingness to "pierce the corporate veil" and attach judgments to the personal assets of officers, directors and shareholders. The reasoning provided by the courts to justify such actions range from the corporation was undercapitalized, to those involved in major decisions were undertaking personal acts of negligence. claims are brought, 3) relatively little of the total loss being paid from liability insurance, 4) defendants winning approximately three-quarters of the cases that reach a verdict, 5) rapidly rising claims and premiums, and 6) most of the money going to lawyers and insurance companies rather than to accident victims.

It is also meaningful to note that a jury system will inherently lend itself to instances of sympathy for the plaintiff. This remains especially true when the individuals asked to serve as jurors come from backgrounds that might more easily identify with the plaintiff. "Any litigant must face the prospect of putting their fate in the hands of disgruntled jurors who are paid at a menial rate and are spending most of their time in wearying idleness."[5] As stated in a Chicago Tribune editorial, "Many who are summoned to jury duty are never called to sit. Many more twiddle their thumbs for days, time taken away from their jobs and homes, before actually serving on a jury. The result may be not only boredom, but a pool of angry, uncooperative people, who feel they have been victimized by the state. This is hardly an ideal frame of mind for a jury."[6] Therefore, under these circumstances, the corporation whether onshore or offshore, is rarely enough. It is, however, usually an important element of planning.

---

[5] Jeffrey O'Connell, "The Lawsuit Lottery", p.84
[6] Chicago Tribune, April 22, 1978, p.8

Deep Pockets

Most attorneys filing a civil judgment on behalf of a client work on a contingency basis. The plaintiff's lawyers will only get paid if they can get a settlement or win the suit. As such, they are not interested in pursuing "judgment proof" defendants. During the normal course of business an attorney will do a financial investigation directed at the target of the litigation. There are numerous services that can be retained that will be able to detail your financial well being. The information available will likely include: your bank accounts, brokerage accounts, property ownership, collectibles, credit rating, business holdings, etc.

"This is well known as the search for the deep pocket defendant. The measure of an attorney's skill is the ability to construct a theory of liability, which will connect a remote and seemingly innocent deep pocket to a particular case. In order to qualify as a deep pocket, it is no longer necessary to be a multimillionaire or to have the resources of a bank, insurance company or public company. As tens of thousands of newly minted lawyers enter into to the fray each year and attempt to earn a living at the litigation game, the standards for admission into the Deep Pocket Club are continually sinking. Now, anyone who has some equity in a home or some retirement savings can be considered as a potential target for a lawsuit."[7]

Since the 1960's the dramatic increase in law school applicants has been tied directly to media exposure. An ample number of stories glamorizing lawyers in television, movies, magazines and other media have appeared. Public awareness has been raised by the exploits of "Perry Mason" to the lifestyle suggested by "LA Law". F.Lee Baily became a national figure with several closely followed cases and his

---

[7] Robert J. Mintz, MBA, JD, "San Diego Business Journal" Vol. 16, no.23 June 5, 1995

book "The Defense Never Rests". Other attorneys would follow, beating a path to the best seller list, all contributing to a litigation explosion. It should come as little surprise that with the combination of a victim mentality by society and an increase in lawyers the system was placed on overload. It is obvious that many currently practicing the profession of law have a vested interest in this litigation explosion. Reform, therefore, seems unlikely. After all, lawyers hold most of the legislative positions. "They're affluent, active and articulate. Also in terms of relative zeal, they have something now that reform would take away, and that gives them a whole different mental set than the rest of us."[8]

So what to do?

"Litigation should be a last resort, not a knee-jerk reflex."
– Irving S. Shapiro

The first and easiest remedy is to keep your financial affairs private. It makes perfect sense. If you are not perceived as offering deep pockets then the likelihood of legal action being taken against you is reduced. An astute person realizes that by lowering one's financial profile, aggressive lawyers who get compensated on a percentage of the client's recovery, will be less likely to target them. The goal then is two fold; lower the client's visibility and protect funds in such a way as not to make them accessible.

Confidentiality is therefore an important element to most asset protection strategies. It can be protected and enhanced by taking several very simple steps. Please keep in mind that any asset protection plan must have a sound legal foundation. You should never attempt to defraud creditors. Quality legal advice should be sought prior to implementing any plan. A few suggestions to increase confidentiality would be:

---

[8] Demkovich, "It's Time for Another Battle on No-Fault Insurance," National Journal Oct. 8, 1977, pp. 1572-73

1)   Keep all documents and correspondence in a secure place.

2)   Share information with only those people that really need to be aware of your affairs. This "need to know" strategy is probably the one most frequently violated.

3)   Utilize the attorney / client privilege with your lawyer to protect sensitive information.

4)   Keep in mind that your attorney is an officer of the court. As such, they are bound by guidelines limiting the duty to promote a client's cause. Your attorney cannot be part of an illegal or fraudulent ascertain. Therefore, if you are hoping for their assistance to "hide" funds offshore, they cannot help you.

5)   There is absolutely no reason to participate in illegal methods to "hide" money. It is one of the quickest ways to jeopardize your confidentiality. There are plenty of legal strategies that can be implemented to protect oneself.

It is important to cite another point pertaining to the client / attorney privilege. It can be waived. This is not always done on purpose. As stated in the superb book, "The Executive's Guide to Business Law", "The attorney / client privilege can generally be asserted at any time and in just about any context. However, it can also be waived, and it can be waived inadvertently. One such example of an inadvertent wavier involved a case where a corporation allowed government investigators to review its files, including privileged communications and another case where a privileged communication was sent outside the control group." [9]

U.S. Judgments Are Not Recognized Offshore

US civil litigation is simply not recognized in many overseas locations. The important word is civil. For example, within the borders of the United States, minor civil violations such as parking tickets often do not have reciprocity from state to state. That is, they do not have give and take regarding those issues.

When an individual transfers assets offshore to a separate and privately held entity, they may have effectively made themselves a much smaller target for such actions. This opens the door to a myriad of potential strategies. If ownership is correctly structured, the ultimate beneficiary of those assets may only be known by the client. By using an offshore entity, assets can be transferred to a legal entity, out of reach by those who would submit frivolous lawsuits. In this scenario, the original transfer of assets is a critical stage and must be carefully planned and carried out. Again, knowledgeable legal council must be used in order to meet all obligations.

---

[9] William A. Hancock, "Executive's Guide to Business Law" p.5-4

Pursuing You Offshore

In the rare event a plaintiff should wish to follow you offshore, they may find it a very expensive and distasteful experience. If your assets have been legally transferred overseas, and ownership of the offshore entity has been structured to capitalize upon asset protection benefits of the jurisdiction of choice, you have tipped the scales in your favor.

For example, in one specific jurisdiction, the plaintiff would need to first know the assets are being held within the country and then retain a local attorney. It would be at considerable expense inasmuch as there is an absence of barristers willing to work on a contingency fee. Also, since frivolous lawsuits are not looked upon favorably, it would be incumbent upon that attorney to convince a local court to hear the case. Even if that can be accomplished, the case will be dismissed should it be proven that assets were transferred prior to the suit being filed. The wicked battle awaiting a plaintiff offshore often results in either a settlement on the defendant's terms or the suit being dropped all together.

Ownership of a Private Bank

It has become apparent that within the existing legal crisis in the United States, anyone of substance is a likely target for a law suit. On the first page of this chapter, a graphic was provided. The ten sources of lawsuits listed provide only a brief synopsis of the numerous reasons for this tremendous increase in spurious litigation. Additionally, a huge domestic trade deficit and debt problem has fueled the fires of government agencies looking for any potential avenues of revenue. Thus, personal privacy is being sacrificed as the Federal Government strives to track the movement of personal assets of citizens.

A Private International Bank can be a significant tool utilized in order to shield your family or business wealth from such probes. It is again important to note that it cannot be used to "hide" money. A captive bank must comply with all reporting regulations. It can, however, be another important layer to an overall blueprint for asset protection.

In addition, the mere fact that a Private International Bank is conducting financial matters makes it easier to obscure ownership capital. This would hold true since in the normal course of business, loans and deposits are made which result in the transfer of currency. This contrasts with similar functions that might be attempted by individuals or corporations. Again, keep in mind we are not suggesting any method of tax evasion. It can be, however, an effective method for discouraging a frivolous lawsuit.

Commonly, a private bank is part of an overall structure that might include offshore trusts and corporations. It is crucial to consult an attorney that specializes in asset protection and has a working knowledge of offshore vehicles before attempting to implement such a plan. Since most attorneys are busy with other aspects of their practice, the exact location of the entities might be best left in the hands of an offshore consulting firm.

Case Study

The following scenario presents a real-life example of a client group who utilized private bank ownership for asset protection and preservation. Through ownership, the group was able to successfully protect both personal and professional assets from potential litigation while additionally exerting a higher degree of control over the movement of those assets.

Please view Figure 2 on the following page.

Figure 2

Case Study:

Prospects Name:	Withheld
Industry:	Wealth Preservation for Individual & Family
Company Name:	Withheld
Company Website:	Withheld
In Business Since:	Withheld

Need:

Asset Protection / Asset Preservation / Control / Privacy
Looking to preserve & protect family assets and ultimately have greater control over them. Would like to consolidate family trusts & set up preparatory measures for future generations' well being. Additionally, seeking increased privacy of personal & professional matters.

Solution:

A Swiss Trust Company (STC) enables its owner to consolidate family trusts under one umbrella through creation of sub-accounts. The STC would increase asset protection and preserve the trust assets for future generations. In addition, the owner of an STC is afforded more control in the movement of funds.

Benefit:

Asset Protection, Asset Preservation, Privacy and Control.

Final Comments:

The client was able to utilize a Swiss Trust Company established in 1936 to accomplish their goals of consolidating family trusts and exerting greater control over the management of assets. Additionally, sub accounts were created which enabled the client to preserve assets for future generations. Through ownership of the Swiss Trust Company both the individual's & family trust assets were protected from potential litigation.

WORLDWIDE BUSINESS CONSULTANTS. *Innovative Offshore Solutions Since 1991.*

WBC
WORLDWIDE
BUSINESS CONSULTANTS

Fraudulent Transfers

The best and safest time to create an asset protection strategy is before there are any potential creditors. If you wait until a lawsuit is pending there is a substantial risk that a court will find any transfer of assets an attempt to defraud. At that point there are serious consequences. A perceived attempt to defraud a creditor would likely result in the setting aside of any transfer.

"Frivolous lawsuits are booming in this county. The U.S. has more costs of litigation per person than any other industrialized nation in the world, and it is crippling our economy."
- Jack Kingston

Conclusion

In modern society the occurrence of frivolous lawsuits is at an all time high and most likely will only continue to grow. Now more than ever, it is essential to protect your assets from the risk of being wiped out in a potential lawsuit. As litigation is now considered a greater threat to wealth than taxes, it is your responsibility to protect yourself. No one else will. For nearly two decades now, the use of offshore vehicles has become a significant aspect of modern estate planning tactics for wealthy individuals and their families. Done legally and ethically, transferring your assets to an offshore entity has the ability to dramatically "tip the scales" in your favor.

Chapter 13

"Your Privacy for Sale"

"There was of course, no way of knowing, whether you were being watched at any given moment. How often, or on what system, the Thought Police plugged in on any individual wire, was guesswork. It was even conceivable that they watched everybody all the time. But at any rate they could plug in your wire whenever they wanted to. You had to live, did live, from habit that became instinct-in the assumption that every sound you made was overheard, and, except in darkness, every movement scrutinized." - George Orwell, 1984

What do you have to hide? If you are like most citizens, the answer is nothing. You work hard, pay your taxes and maintain a clean slate. Your main concerns are family, a home and maybe a luxury item that you allow yourself from time to time. Whether you are considered middle class, upper middle class or financially independent, the odds of your personal privacy being violated on a daily basis probably seems remote. Those who seem concerned with such issues, most likely appear to either be paranoid or involved in illegal activity.

The facts however, paint an entirely different picture. In an age of computers and other sophisticated devices, your privacy has virtually gone the way of "Packman". Your most sensitive, personal information has a price tag on it and is sitting, for all practical purposes, on the shelf at your local computer store. Current laws are incapable of keeping pace with the technological advances occurring in our society. Like most rights or privileges, once left unprotected, your privacy is easily lost. So, for those productive citizens with nothing to hide, this black-market can create a very uncomfortable feeling of being violated. Even worse, it can cost substantial sums of money should a thief obtain information such as bank account numbers, credit card numbers or other personal data. The strides that computer hackers and other unscrupulous individuals have made against privacy are so vast that a "privacy bill of rights" has been discussed by the United States Congress.

As recently as 2006, Senator Hillary Clinton called for a comprehensive privacy agenda again including the need for a "privacy bill of rights." Senator Clinton expressed her perspective on privacy stating, "At all levels, the privacy protections for ordinary Americans are broken, inadequate and out of date. It's time for a new comprehensive look at privacy. We need consumer protections that are up to date with the technological and national security needs of our time, for a world in which we can be confident that our security and our privacy are both protected."[1]

Whether or not Congress will ever take this issue seriously is a matter for debate. It has been almost twenty years since the "Code of Fair Information Practices" was reviewed. In addition, United States telecommunications laws have not undergone a major underwrite since 1934.

A Constitutional Amendment
"The right of the people to be secure in their persons, houses and effects, and against unreasonable searches and seizures, shall not be violated, and no warrant shall issue, but upon probable cause, supported by oath or affimation,

---

[1] Senator Hillary Rodham Clinton Online. Retrieved on November 21, 2008.

and particularly describing the place to be searched, and the person or things to be seized." -Fourth Amendment to the United States Constitution

The right to privacy is one of the most basic and natural rights, which is why it is also the most essential to citizens of the United States. Nobody is perfect, by virtue of the human condition, we make mistakes. Some are so colossal that they can never truly be placed in the past. Most are not. You have a basic human right not to be compelled to consistently relive your transgressions. Take a moment and think. How many of us can really say our life is an open book? How many would want to do so?

Privacy for Profit

The motive behind violating someone's personal privacy is not gossip, it's money. For the most part, those in tune to your private matters are total strangers. This has become a multi-billion dollar industry with little in the way of checks and balances. The damages being done are subtle, quickly accomplished and not usually detected until much later. It is now possible to break into your home from a computer 3,000 miles away and leave little in the way of evidence. The information being taken can include everything from how much money you make, your medical records, social security numbers, phone call history, purchasing habits, credit card numbers, credit history, cars owned or leased, pets registered, names & ages of children and much more; the list is infinite. In a few extreme documented cases, stalkers have enlisted private information brokers to obtain the home addresses of famous individuals. The results can be tragic.

Your impression should not be that this is happening in isolated instances. You can virtually be guaranteed that during the course of reading this chapter, someone unknown to you, and without your permission, has accessed privileged information. Found in many different forms, these types of unauthorized accesses to information can be as easy as cross-referencing an 800 or 900 phone number that you recently called, to obtain your address. Yes, you can bet that if you responded to an advertisement with those prefixes, that your name, address and phone number will be coded with the product or service as a registered interest and then later sold. Did you ever wonder how you received blind solicitations from companies for a hobby or personal interest? The person accessing your information may be doing it for much more ominous reasons.

"Privacy is not something that I'm merely entitled to, it's an absolute prerequisite."
- Marlon Brando

Recent statistics show that one of every four Americans has been victim to Identity Theft, one of the most severe types of privacy violations. Your social security number in the hands of a knowledgeable thief can have devastating results. False identities can be established, credit cards used and bank accounts closed. USA Today found that, "over 10 million people fell victim to identity theft in recent years with estimated losses of $5 billion out of pocket and more than $48 billion in losses to businesses and financial institutions."[2]

Selling Information

Selling information is a growing industry. Any list of information merchants starts with the traditional sellers using conventional sources, such as major credit card companies. As much information as they have, or can get, is sold to third party vendors. Credit Bureaus are also in the business of selling information, and maybe most shockingly, a new player has evolved into this

---

[2] USA Today Online "Federal survey: Identity theft statistics show 1 in 4 hit in U.S. households" Retrieved on November 21, 2008.

marketplace. State and local governments, who many citizens regard as protectors of privileged information, are now engaging themselves in the business of selling data. Cash hungry governments are selling information pertaining to civil filings, court records, traffic ticket information, voter registration, property rolls, etc. This data is being sold to "information brokers" for resale to anyone willing to pay. It has been recently estimated that the US Government maintains 16 files for every man, woman and child living in the United States. With a population of over 245 million that information base has reached an incredible level. The list of those willing to purchase such information include: attorneys, collectors, investigators or even potential employers and creditors.

Freedom is the ability to live life in peace without undo intrusions by government agencies, bureaucrats or others that have their own self-interests and agendas. Excessive government is frequently a sign of weakness. Blocked accounts, currency restrictions and confiscation of property are usually a last resort. A bureaucrat engaging in direct intimidation is doing so out of fear and in an attempt to protect a power base.

Privacy Violations
History is filled with examples of governments invading the privacy of its citizens. With the line between legally obtained data and intrusion blurred, action is needed. The problem will continue to exponentially grow without preventive steps. There is a very important point to be made here: it is up to the individual to protect their own privacy rights. We as members of this society can not blindly depend upon any faceless government body to accomplish this for us.

In 1914, the Supreme Court heard Weeks v. United States, a case concerning the search and seizure of items at a private residence. Evidence gathered against Fremont Weeks proved that he was selling lottery tickets by mail, violating anti-gambling laws in the state of Missouri. The Supreme Court, however, determined that the evidence was gathered illegally, violating Fourth Amendment protections, and therefore could not be used as evidence in a court of law.

"The Fifth Amendment is an old friend and a good friend. It is one of the great landmarks in men's struggle to be free of tyranny, to be decent and civilized."
- Justice William O. Douglas

The question of what constitutes illegal search and seizure has blurred as property is no longer just physical but often electronic. Well before the development of the Internet, the Supreme Court heard the case of Olmstead v. United States in 1928. In this case, Roy Olmstead was accused of illegally producing and selling alcohol during the period of prohibition. While none of his physical property was searched, Olmstead's private phone conversations were wire tapped and used as evidence in the case. The Supreme Court found in favor of the People, declaring that the Fourth Amendment was not violated as nothing was physically searched or seized. In a now famous dissenting opinion, Associate Justice Louis Brandeis logically assumed that the Fourth Amendment should be expanded to include telephone conversations. He noted at the time the Amendment was written, the only means to search was by violent physical intrusion; however, with the advent of technology, illegal search would need to be defined much more broadly.

As early as 1928, Americans have factored in changing technology with new definitions of illegal search. Today, computers are regularly confiscated in investigations to track web browsing history, emails, bank records and much more. We open ourselves to public eye when we create electronic profiles through our personal websites, social and professional networking sites. We shop online, we bank online, we pay bills online, and each time we do so we leave our records vulnerable to search by both government agencies and criminal predators. Generally, the increased ability to gather and send information has had negative implications for retaining privacy. As large scale information systems become more common, there is so much information stored in many databases worldwide that an individual has no way of knowing of or controlling all of the information about themselves that others may have access to. Such information could potentially be sold to others for profit and/or be used for purposes not known to the individual of which the information is about.

Protecting your Privacy
In addition to the prominent benefits of increased profit and asset protection, the ability to obtain a higher degree of privacy is greatly afforded to owners of private financialinstitutions. Features of offshore banks and trust companies that contribute to increased privacy include anonymous ownership, specialized permits, anonymity of investors and, overall, the ability to control your finances without the use of a third party.

Anonymous ownership is a rare possibility, but the stock certificates of certain types of international companies may be issued in bearer shares, meaning they are not subject to the guidelines of registered shares because ownership is rarely recorded. When the option to own a company anonymously is available, the acquisition will consistently lead to a considerable increase in financial privacy.

Similar to bearer shares, specialized financial services permits are not afforded to all types of offshore companies, but they can often lead to greater privacy for the clients and associates of offshore companies when available. For example, obtaining a Self Regulating Organization (SRO) permit allows a Swiss Trust Company to act as a domestic intermediary for carrying out financial transactions. Those private companies with an SRO permit, typically do not need to disclose client information to a regulating authority. Specialized permits like the SRO will significantly increase the privacy a company can offer to its associates and investors.

If a private company or bank is able to carry out transactions for itself, such as wire transfers or SWIFT transfers, then it will lower its overall financial profile. Lowering a financial profile offers privacy on two fronts: one, the company or bank will be subject to less probes by other financial or governing bodies; two, the individual owners will reduce the appearance of "deep-pockets" that may lead to frivolous law suits.

Under the two major privacy steps of, one, offering anonymity to owners and clients and, two, carrying out transactions without a third party, there are many other nuanced steps to be taken to decrease financial transparency. By making privacy a priority when you acquire, you and your advisors will create a business plan that allows you to keep your financial holdings and transactions a matter of personal record.

Case Study

The following scenario presents a real-life example of a client group who utilized ownership of a Swiss Trust Company to increase their personal privacy as well as the privacy of their Real Estate investors. Through ownership, the group was able to successfully increase their profit while offering non-disclosure of investments from their private investors.

Please view Figure 3 on the following page.

Figure 3

Case Study - Inbound Real Estate:

Prospects Name:	Withheld
Industry:	U.S. Real Estate Development/Investment (Inbound) (Overseas investors to develop in U.S.)
Company Name:	Withheld
Company Website:	Withheld
In Business Since:	Withheld

Need:

Privacy / Profit / Asset Protection
Looking to raise capital from overseas private investors and clients to fund real estate developments in the United States. Seeks general asset protection, asset protection for specific real estate holdings and to protect the privacy of international investors.

Solution:

A Swiss Trust Company (STC) enables its owner to raise capital from overseas investors and offer non-disclosure for those investments. In addition, an STC can encumber property through loans from the STC to United States' companies while ultimately providing asset protection for real estate holdings.

Benefit:

Increased profit, privacy and asset protection.

Final Comments:

The Real Estate group was able to achieve its goals through ownership of a Swiss Trust Company established in 1968. The privacy of investors was protected and asset protection was provided to both the developers and investors. Through an STC, this group was able to profit substantially from raising funds overseas and capitalizing on the U.S. real estate market & the weak dollar. Furthermore, this group was afforded a competitive edge in the goodwill associated with the prestige of an STC established in 1968.

WORLDWIDE BUSINESS CONSULTANTS. *Innovative Offshore Solutions Since 1991.*

"We must protect our citizens' privacy -- the bulwark of personal liberty, the safeguard of individual creativity."
- Former President Bill Clinton

Conclusion

The right to privacy is one of the most essential and natural rights given to American citizens and as such, the need to protect it is vital. While advances in modern technology have made our daily lives much easier, these advances have also opened all U.S. citizens to a higher threat of becoming victim to potential privacy violations. Simple steps can and must be taken to ensure that your privacy, in any of its many forms, is not breached.

Chapter 14

"Questions You Should Ask When Considering an Acquisition"

As with any subject, when researching the acquisition or establishment of a private financial institution, you should formulate concise and informative questions. The information derived from these questions will assist in determining whether or not this arena is a viable alternative for your needs. This section is comprised of the most commonly asked questions and responses, and should be a solid platform from which to begin your initial stages of due-diligence.

Q. Which country would be best suited for my needs?
A. One should first determine what they want to accomplish with the acquisition then research which jurisdictions offer a compatible license. The next step is to familiarize yourself with the qualification process and paid-in capital requirements. Licensing fees, legal fees and capitalization requirements vary considerably when comparing countries.

Q. Which countries should I avoid?
A. Other than countries that simply do not offer the type of license you desire, there are jurisdictions that are being misrepresented in connection with what their legislation actually offers. Be certain that you are dealing with a reputable and knowledgeable agent who offers familiar alternatives, as well as the more obscure, but credible, locations.

Q. What are the qualification requirements?
A. Qualification for ownership generally focuses on the moral character and financial suitability of the individual

or group. The applicant must be prepared to submit business and bank references, audited financials, a criminal clearance report and a personal resume.

Q. *Are there minimum capitalization requirements?*

A. Dependent upon the type (or class) of financial institution under consideration, there are indeed minimum capital requirements over and above the initial investment for the acquisition. Deposits may range from US$100,000 up to US$1million which may be held in cash or liquid securities. While some countries' legislation allows for the capital to be held in major banks and brokerages throughout the world, others require the funds be deposited with a domestic institution such as a national or central bank.

Q. *Does ownership require previous experience?*

A. In many cases, the owners of a financial institution do not need to have banking and extensive financial expertise. Directors and other bank officers, however, must supply sufficient proof of a diverse background in both banking and finance. In many cases, Directors, Secretaries and other administrative personnel may be hired at reasonable rates.

Q. *Will my funds be safe?*

A. An offshore financial institution will normally establish depository and correspondent accounts with major international banking and brokerage institutions. It is suggested that the private international bank owner maintain sole signatory power of the accounts. A separate discretionary account, for example, maintained with a minimal balance, may be desirable if contracting offshore management.

Q. *How accessible are my funds?*

A. In addition to establishing checking or depository accounts with major financial institutions, as previously mentioned, the owner may want to inquire as to the availability of wire transfer withdrawals via faxed instructions from the signatory. One other option is to become a member of the Society for Worldwide Interbank Financial Telecommunication (SWIFT) or EuroClear.

Q. *Can I invest in US Government Securities?*

A. Yes, dependent upon the brokerage house(s) you choose, you may be able to invest in securities both foreign and domestic.

Q. *Am I protected against lawsuits?*

A. A private financial institution will be held responsible for its operations and must adhere to the legislative guidelines of its country of domicile as well as any other country in which it may conduct business. Otherwise, the institution may risk legal ramifications and the possible revocation of its license. However, in most cases it is difficult to initiate a lawsuit or receive a judgment against a private institution without first persuading the host government to conduct their own investigation. With even the most incriminating evidence, one may find this to be an extremely onerous and expensive process. In addition, private owners may shield their personal assets with an Asset Protection Trust, a vehicle that can be virtually impenetrable if properly structured.

Q. *Are there tax advantages?*

A. While each country has its own tax legislation and structuring, you may want to consider a tax haven jurisdiction. There are many such countries that do not impose income tax, capital tax, stamp duty, death duty, state duty, gift duty or any other taxes or duties of like nature. Your own personal tax obligations would be determined by the legislation of the government where you are considered a citizen, and will most likely be related to dividends realized from the financial institution's profits. (It is suggested that you consult a certified accountant, familiar with offshore business, regarding these matters).

Q. *Can an offshore financial institution make personal loans?*
A. Yes, as long as the institution is authorized to contract personal loans within its memorandum and articles of association.

Q. *Can the financial institution advertise and solicit business?*
A. Yes, once again, if it is deemed appropriate for the type of institution in question. In addition to the domicile of your institution, you must also consider the regulations pertaining to this subject matter in the countries in which you anticipate advertising or soliciting.

Q. *Is administrative and management assistance available?*
A. There are a variety of companies that are able to assist with the operations of an offshore financial institution. Expertise in financial functions and the range of services offered will vary. The cost is basically determined by the amount of activity of the particular facility and to what extent the role of manager or administrator will be. The annual cost could begin as low as US$5,000.

Q. *How can I trust my overseas representatives?*
A. It is suggested that you are referred to a representative by someone you trust to be knowledgeable in this field. You may also want to conduct your own due-diligence by requesting references and background information. In any case, you must proceed in the relationship cautiously, and if you deem it necessary to allow the representative to access funds, you may consider establishing a discretionary account, as mentioned previously.

Q. Who most frequently purchases private financial institutions?
A. The popularity of private, international financial institutions has been steadily increasing since the mid-seventies when it was considered to be widely introduced to the private sector. What initially seemed to be reserved for the financial elite became more prevalent around this time with groups and individuals of more modest means.

This holds even truer today. In fact, with the broadening of the international marketplace in Europe and Southeast Asia, the importance of establishing oneself offshore is becoming more obvious to those even remotely involved in the international arena. From smaller import/export companies to major financial conglomerates, offshore banking is not simply gaining in popularity and acceptability but becoming a necessity in some circles. This is not to imply that everyone should consider owning a private institution, most would not qualify or have the financial need. For a select few, however, it is an invaluable tool.

Q. How long is the process of acquiring an institution?
A. There are many opportunities available ranging in timeframes from nearly immediate to more lengthy processes of a year or more. You should discuss your time frame expectations with a professional who will locate opportunities in line with those goals.

Q. What is a Trust Company?
A. A Trust Company, like a bank, is financial institution. It is important to note that a Trust Company is not an actual bank but can provide many banking services. Also, not to be confused with Special Purpose Trusts, a Trust Company can provide a wide variety of fiduciary and administrative services to shareholders, related subsidiaries and clients.

Q. What is the actual authority of a Trust Company?

A. The primary objectives of Trust Companies are to provide lending, portfolio management, credit card processing, insurance brokerage, real estate brokerage and other trust and fiduciary services listed at length throughout our firm's website

Q. What services can I provide through owning a Private Bank?

A. The powers of a Private Bank are vast and listed in full detail within our Bank Acquisition Highlights section of this website. A few powers of Private Banks include, the ability to issue letters of credit, credit and debit card processing, the creation of correspondent banking relationships worldwide and many more.

Q. What is the major use of a Captive Insurance Company?

A. A Captive Insurance Company is an institution established primarily as a risk management technique that enables its owner(s) to finance retained losses in a formal structure. Additionally, a Captive Insurance Company can be used for reinsurance purposes in addition to issuing insurance to protect employers and principals from various risks.

In conclusion, we recommend discussing ownership of a private bank or Trust Company with all decision makers within your organization including your legal and financial advisors. In any conversation regarding your acquisition, be wary of claims of tax relief.

Chapter 15

"Fact vs. Fiction"

No informative work would be complete without some mention of the colorful characters and "exclusive offers" one can encounter when looking offshore. In our estimation, the following issues must be brought to your attention. In order to fulfill this obligation, it is incumbent upon us to strongly suggest extreme caution in any dealings with these people or any other misleading offers that may sound "too good to be true". The advent of the internet has resulted in a huge increase in computer-related scams typically associated with personal information and identity theft.

Although the offshore market is a wonderful place filled with great opportunities, it is, however, without central regulation. Therefore, it can resemble the United States' wild west of the mid nineteenth century. Fortunes are made but guidance is often imperative. In this chapter, we will highlight a few of the most notorious offshore scams and other, lesser-known fraudulent offers around today. Additionally, we will provide an overview of a few true stories that relate to the offshore marketplace.

Scams

1) *Melchizedek*
The ecclesiastical sovereignty of Melchizedek is a self-proclaimed micro-nation that has been attempting to establish itself as an international financial center for years. To our knowledge, the so-called "Dominion of Melchizedek" is NOT recognized by the United Nations nor any other first

world nation. Conflicting reports make it difficult to capture the entire history of the Dominion of Melchizedek, although it was said to be created in 1986 by Evan David Pedley and his son, Mark Logan Pedley. Dejure recognition, however, was apparently extended by a third world UN member on June 3, 1993. We do not know the terms of this recognition, nor pretend to understand its significance. In addition, Melchizedek also claims to have their own Embassy in Washington DC. If this is so, they have done this without the approval of the United States Government. Finally, although ownership claims have been made to several islands, no physical presence has been established anywhere in the world.

For now, the Dominion has recorded their territorial claims to the island of Malpelo, which is a few hundred miles off the coast of Colombia, and the island of Clipperton, which is several hundred miles off the Pacific coast of Southern Mexico. To substantiate their claims they often cite the Wellington Convention which met more than fifty years ago. It is their assertion that UN members were forbidden from claiming these previously unclaimed islands. Melchizedek's originators suggest that the Convention allowed for the islands mentioned to be considered open territory for Melchizedek, or any legitimate government, to take advantage of the political possibilities available. The governments of Mexico and Colombia feel differently.

If the "Dominion" was successful in its goal of becoming a widely accredited nation, it would enjoy the benefits of being recognized by other world nations and profit from the interaction of business and commerce. In addition, Melchizedek would be able to issue credible licenses for banks, mutual funds and corporations.

In September of 1996, the Texas Department of Insurance issued a cease-and-desist order halting, what they termed an "illegal bond business". An unlicensed Houston guaranty bond operation, headed by a man claiming to be ex-president of the Dominion of Melchizedek. Insurance Commissioner Elton Bomer stated "Investigators for the Texas Department of Insurance's Fraud Unit have been unable to locate any legitimate country under the title Dominion of Melchizedek. Besides shutting down this operation, TDI is turning over all information on the case to the proper legal authorities." The Department supported their position with affidavits from Federal government officials, including John Shockey, head of the fraud unit of the US Comptroller of the Currency. They also cited an article that ran November 5, 1995 in the Washington Post calling it a nonexistent country. [1]

Over the last decade, Melchizedek has periodically been issuing licenses for banks and other financial entities from a myriad of agents throughout the United States, Canada and Europe. Banks at one time were being offered for sale at $60,000. These agents claimed that you can establish an entity with the term "Bank" in the title with no qualification requirements necessary. Melchizedek will impose no taxation, will issue bearer shares and offer immediate delivery. No reputable country, in our opinion, would allow the establishment of such an entity under these circumstances. In addition, it seems highly unlikely that any reputable financial center or institution would recognize the authority or viability of these entities.

It must be noted that the Dominion of Melchizedek does offer a response to many of these reports by major

---

[1] www.tdi.state.tx.us

periodicals and disputes the facts. For more information and take a look at their website at *www.melchizedek.com*

Developments reported on their site include the following news releases:

- May 31, 1998 DOM at this time refrains from declaring "spiritual war" on Pakistan and India.
- June 3, 1998 Melchizedek declares "spiritual war" on Serbia.

2) *Starting Your Own Country*

Scams similar to that of Melchizedek can include any types of misleading offers to "start your own county." Commonly, these countries can take place underwater, far-off mythical lands or strictly on the internet. By definition, these countries are considered "micronations," meaning they are an "entity created and maintained as if it were a nation and/or a state, and generally carrying with it some, most or all of the attributes of nationhood, and likewise generally carrying with it some of the attributes of statehood. Though a micronation may well have begun as a mere drollery, it has the potential (given the evolution of a sufficiently vital national culture) to develop into a true nation, and possibly to achieve statehood." [2]

Marketed as a "great investment" opportunity, micronations usually hold little or no land, but lay claim to sovereign independence and territory. Most are unrecognized by the major countries of the world as they are attempts at founding new countries. They often declare dominion over land that actually exists, often tiny, isolated islands, or other areas undeveloped by major world powers. Like other countries, many Micronations have proclaimed declarations of independence,

---

[2] "How to Start Your Own Country" geocities.com Retrieved November 2008.

adopted constitutions, sought diplomatic recognition, appointed ambassadors, displayed national flags, and issued stamps, passports, and currency.

Any search online will pull up a long list of these far off vacation-like destinations. Some micronations worthy of note aside from the Dominion of Melchizedek include: Oceania, The Atlantis Project, a floating sea-city, The Kingdom of TorHavn the world's first "green" country, The Kingdom of Talossa, the Republic of Freedonia and many more.

3) *Nigerian Scam*

For nearly ten years, the Nigerian "advanced fee" scam has been running uninterrupted and as far as we can tell, there is no end in sight. The scam operates as follows: The target receives an unsolicited email or fax from a Nigerian contact. Often they approach you, claiming that your standing in the community has given them reason to believe that you could be of assistance. The letter is frequently from a non-existent entity called the Nigerian Oil Corporation. The pitch is to help them get money out of Nigeria for which a huge fee would be paid to you, usually in the millions. They will request that you either pay an "advanced fee" to help smooth the way for the transaction or provide them with copies of your letterhead. They of course will need your banking coordinates to finalize the transaction. Once this information is in hand, the confidence man will attempt to clean out your bank account. If an advanced fee is paid, they are never shy and will invariably claim to have problems with the transaction. More money of course would cure everything.

There are many variations to this scam. We highly suggest consulting the US State Department and the Nigerian Embassy for additional information.

4) *Prime Bank Guarantess*

Another scam dating many years back, relates to Prime Bank Fraud. Just when this scam appears to have died down, it unexpectedly flares back up. The advent of the internet has enabled this scam to expand significantly attracting a much larger audience than in previous years. Both the Securities Exchange Commission and the International Chamber of Commerce have posted numerous warnings related to this scam.

Prime bank programs often claim investors' funds will be used to purchase and trade "prime bank" financial instruments on clandestine overseas markets in order to generate huge returns in which the investor will share. However, neither these instruments, nor the markets on which they allegedly trade, exist.

A few warning signs of prime banking fraud according to the Securities and Exchange Commission include:

- *Excessive Guaranteed Returns:*
These fraudulent investment pitches typically offer or guarantee spectacular returns of 20 to 200 percent monthly, absolutely risk free. Promises of unrealistic returns at no risk are hallmarks of prime bank fraud.

- *Fictitious Financial Instrument:*
Despite having credible-sounding names, the supposed "financial instruments" at the heart of any prime bank scheme simply do not exist.

- *Extreme Secrecy:*
Promoters claim that transactions must be kept strictly confidential by all parties, making client references unavailable. They may characterize the transactions as the best-kept secret in the banking industry, and assert that, if asked, bank and regulatory officials would deny knowledge of such instruments. Investors may be asked to sign nondisclosure agreements.

- *Exclusive Opportunity:*
Promoters frequently claim that investment opportunities of this type are by invitation only, available to only a handful of special customers, and historically reserved for the wealthy elite.
- *Claims of Inordinate Complexity:*
Investment pitches frequently are vague about who is involved in the transaction or where the money is going. Promoters may try to explain away this lack of specificity by stating that the financial instruments are too technical or complex for nonexperts to understand.

Additional Scams Worthy of Note

The Black Money Scam
Also known as the 'wash wash scam', is a scam where con artists attempt to fraudulently obtain money from a victim by persuading him or her that piles of banknote-sized paper in a trunk or a safe is really money which has been dyed black (e.g. to avoid detection by customs). The victim is persuaded to pay for chemicals to wash the "money" with a promise that he will share in the proceeds. The black money scam first appeared around the year 2000.

The Russian Dating Scam
Specifically targeting U.S. citizens, this scam has grown in recent years due to the internet. United States citizens should be alert to attempts at fraud by persons claiming to live in Russia professing friendship, romantic interest, and /or marriage intentions over the Internet. Typically, once a connection is made, the correspondent asks the U.S. citizen to send money or credit card information for living expenses, travel expenses, or "visa costs". Sometimes, the correspondent notifies the American citizen that a close family member, usually the mother, is in desperate need of

surgery and begins to request monetary assistance. Scams have even advanced to the point where the U.S. citizen is informed of a serious or fatal accident to the correspondent and the "family" asks for money to cover hospital or funeral costs. This scam has amassed great financial losses to many victims of it.

Additional variations on this type can come from any overseas country and usually involve online dating communities, social networking sites or online chat rooms. It is essential to be aware of scams such as this if you are an active online user.

The Spanish Lottery Scam

The United States Embassy in Madrid, receives frequent inquiries about the Spanish Lottery (sometimes referred to as "El Gordo"). Most inquiries result in complaints in regards to a scam in which purported Spanish lottery officials inform victims that they have won a large cash prize. This scam is just another example of the many advance-fee cons being run around the world.

First, the victim receives an "award confirmation" through fax or email informing them that they have won a large amount of money in a Spanish lottery drawing. "Due to a clerical error" or some other sort of mix-up, the winner is asked to keep his or her prize confidential until the winnings are released to them. Most times, there is a deadline to claim the money. Once the "transfer process" begins, the victim is informed of various delays requiring the payment of transfer fees, taxes, anti-terror fees, insurance fees, claims agent fees, and other administrative costs that they must pay before the prize can officially be collected. This scam runs under many different seemingly official names such as "El Gordo Sweepstakes Lottery" or actual lottery names such as "Once."

True Story: **"No Entry"**

Did you know that certain overseas newspapers are strongly discouraged from entry into the United States? It's true. Even if you wish to subscribe to the periodical, it may be impossible to do so and receive it in the States. The reason has to do with the type of advertisement being placed. The United States is highly regulated for newspapers that advertise overseas bank rates and securities markets. By protecting its citizens, regulators also extremely limit the amount of information entering the US pertaining to overseas investment.

True Story: **"So you must be hiding money"**

A loyal US bank customer instructed their branch manager to prepare a wire transfer to the Union Bank of Switzerland. The bank's client had a history of over ten years with their institution, a fine reputation and considered a leading business person within the community. The branch manager, who should be sophisticated in financial matters, offers the following insight. "So you must be trying to hide money." His comment was not made in jest. The account was moved to another bank shortly thereafter.

True Story: **"Offshore in Oklahoma"**

An offshore bank in Oklahoma? An attempt has been made to do just that. Native Americans are hoping to take advantage of tribal agreements with the United States Federal Government. "Broadly written, tribal-sovereignty laws put Native Americans in the unique position of being the only Americans who can basically tell the government to get lost." [3]

First Lenape National Bank of Anadarko, Oklahoma has attempted to offer banking privacy while still on the mainland of the United States. "That means numbered

---

[3] Geoff Colvin, "Fortune Magazine", June 20, 1997

accounts, full nondisclosure of account information, no compliance with snooping law enforcement, protection from civil court judgments and no reporting of interest to the IRS or of cash deposits over $10,000 to the Treasury Department. First Lenape is owned by the Delaware tribe of western Oklahoma, a sovereign Indian nation independent from US authority."[4]

Much remains to be resolved with this issue. The Federal Government is obviously concerned. "The Office of the Comptroller of the Currency, the federal agency that charters and regulates some 3,000 member banks abruptly issued a stern warning."[5] In effect, they hastily scared off potential corresponding banks.

Conclusion

As with any legitimately profitable endeavor such as "going offshore" there are those individuals who seek to take advantage of the un-informed. It is essential to do your research prior to engaging in any type of business endeavor. As you can see from this chapter, the amount of scams related to the offshore marketplace are plentiful and will only continue to grow as more US citizens seek to reap the benefits that can be legally and ethically attained offshore.

Unfortunately, with the technological advances of the internet, the ease for con artists to find victims to scam has grown significantly. Any basic online search will provide a never-ending list of domestic and overseas scams of which to avoid. Organizations such as the Better Business Bureau, the International Chamber of Commerce and the U.S. Department of State all offer their expertise into this complex and costly world of fraud.

---

[4] Ibid
[5] Ibid

Chapter 16

"Final Thoughts"

Over the past two decades, the offshore market has experienced a significant increase in popularity as more Americans have begun to see the vast benefits associated with it. Now more than ever, the need to diversify offshore has become commonplace in furthering business interests while protecting personal wealth. Increased profit, privacy and asset protection are all thoroughly attainable to owners or investors of a private financial institution.

Ownership of a Private Bank or Trust Company is not a get rich quick scheme. It is however, an entrepreneurial endeavor that offers some of the largest profit margins of any business or profession. Correctly done, it provides greater control and profit. Furthermore, it is a wonderful tool used to open markets, enhance status and lower the cost of doing international business.

It is essential, to again point out the fact that owning an offshore financial institution is not a tax shelter. Unfortunately, there are those, who seek to take advantage of the un-informed and would tell you otherwise. Misleading offers from these unethical individuals appear as "treasure chests" of secrets or somewhat comical and elaborately structured scenarios. All of which are supposed to keep the tax man at bay and offer you increased privacy. In these ambiguous situations, it is important to follow the old adage of "if it sounds too good to be true, it probably is."

Overall, the offshore industry and private banking in particular have almost limitless avenues to explore. Within the confines of this format, however, it would be impractical to attempt to create an all encompassing body of work. Our goal was simply to offer an overview of the history and current conditions of the offshore market, the benefits afforded to those who go offshore and an understanding of the potential schemes associated with this industry, all the while lending our expertise in this arena. We hope that was accomplished.

Most importantly, our hope is that you found this to be an informative and enjoyable read. If you would like to explore the concept further, we invite you to call our Los Angeles office at **800-733-2191** or **310-376-3480.**

Worldwide Business Consultants provides ownership opportunities of Private Financial Institutions in over 50 countries worldwide. Each institution offered is run through a strict due diligence process to ensure goodwill & credibility. We leverage our 17 years experience in the field of private acquisitions along with our international resources to offer clients innovative offshore solutions to their individual business problems.

Acknowledgments

We offer our sincerest gratitude to those members of our staff who helped contribute to this endeavor. Without their hard work and dedication, this book would not have been possible.

Ms. Angie Cervantes

Ms. Eva Comeau

Ms. Bethany Henderson

Ms. Alexandra Stauber

www.ingramcontent.com/pod-product-compliance
Lightning Source LLC
Chambersburg PA
CBHW031950170526
45157CB00002B/451